Rosie O'Donnell's

Crafty.U

100 easy projects the whole family
can enjoy all year long

for my mother —
a very crafty woman

Simon & Schuster
1230 Avenue of the Americas
New York, NY 10020

First Simon & Schuster hardcover edition April 2008

SIMON & SCHUSTER and colophon are registered
trademarks of Simon & Schuster, Inc.

For information about special discounts for bulk purchases,
please contact Simon & Schuster Special Sales
at 1-800-456-6798 or business@simonandschuster.com

Designed by Doug Turshen with David Huang

Printed in China

10 9 8 7 6 5 4 3 2 1

Library of Congress Cataloging-in-Publication Data

O'Donnell, Rosie.
  Rosie O'Donnell's crafty U : 100 easy projects the whole
    family can enjoy all year long / Rosie O'Donnell.
      p. cm.
    1. Handicraft. I. Title.

TT157.O32 2008
745.5--dc22   2007031249

ISBN-13: 978-1-4165-5341-0
ISBN-10: 1-4165-5341-X

chillin' on a **SUMMER** day

welcome to
Rosie's **CRAFT CORNER**

jump up! it's **SPRING**

EVERY DAY is
a decoupage day

FALL fun for everyone

lots to do in
WINTER

RAINY DAY
playdate

Welcome to Rosie's Craft Corner

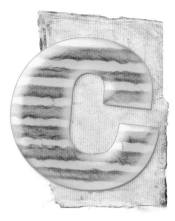

rafts are my way of relaxing. My friends say they can tell how stressed I am by the number of craft projects I'm working on. I find nothing is more soothing than sitting at my craft table with music blaring as loud as the speakers can take—creating. I know I am not alone, many people share my love for crafting, and this book is dedicated to them.

I have enlisted the help of fellow crafter and friend Bobby Pearce, and we've compiled some of our favorite projects. We have carefully designed **CRAFTY U** to be fun for the entire family. In fact, that is exactly why I am doing this book—to inspire families to spend more time together—crafting!

u r crafty – i swear – u r

Many of the projects are super-simple, and many require materials you already have lying around the house. We've organized most of this book by season, but truthfully, you can do lots of these activities any day of the year.

I encourage you to experiment and adapt these projects to create your own crafts. There is plenty of room to express yourself and create your own works of art. We are only limited by our imaginations.

I hope you enjoy **CRAFTY U** as much as I've enjoyed putting it together for you.

this is not a college – but a university
pick ur classes
get urself a degree
i know inside there is a crafty u
u r art

Kids & Crafts

A craft project is a great way for children to explore their creativity, build confidence, and learn how to express themselves. Doing crafts gives them a real sense of accomplishment: There is no better feeling in the world than when someone admires what you've made, and this is a wonderful gift to give a child. You benefit too: Crafts give you a whole other arena in which to have fun with your family.

And fun is the operative word here; perfection is not. Sometimes a project doesn't look exactly like the picture in a book, but so what! A simple rule to follow: If your kids think it's great, it is. Help them to see that. Comment on what makes their project unique, and encourage them to add their own special touches. In many cases, you and your children should follow our instructions closely to avoid a big mess, but you can still show them ways to personalize their work. Color is a good place to start. A project may call for a red star, but who says it can't be blue? Support your little artists in making these decisions so they enjoy the creative process.

You can learn a lot about your kids along the way. Ask questions and encourage them to interpret the work. Maybe they'd like to explain why they used a certain color or to describe their design on a mosaic. The best thing to do is to get them to talk, and then pay attention to their responses.

Of course, it's important to be prepared for a project before you get the kids involved—and we've put together a resource guide so you can find what you need (Best Places for Craft Supplies, page 204). But feel free to improvise with what you already have around your house: If you don't have polka-dot stickers, for example, use what's on hand or make your own (see page 198 for our recipe for Sticker Glue!). Be spontaneous!

The final step is showing off what's been created—and kids love the feedback. Set up a special area in your house where work is displayed, and when friends and other family members come over, take them into "the gallery" and show it off. Above all, let your children know how much you appreciate their talent. Get in the habit of putting up new work often to get kids excited about future projects. Also, date the back of the project and jot down a few words about it. (Twenty years from now, you'll be happy you took the time!)

Creating Your Own Craft Corner

A spare bedroom or extra space in a garage or laundry room is ideal, but you can create an area for crafts with just a kitchen table along with a few empty drawers or shelves for storing supplies.

The first thing to consider is where to set up your craft area. Find a spot that is easy to get to, has adequate workspace, and is situated in a well-ventilated room, because you'll be working with paint and glue. One basic rule: If it smells, it's probably not good for you, so open a window. A small fan helps keep fumes away.

Lighting is important. Make sure you can see properly. The best way to view color is in natural light, but if sunlight is not available, a clear white bulb provides even illumination. Soft lights and pink-hued bulbs will not give you an accurate view of color. If you are working on a project where color matching is important, take it outside or to a window and view the color in sunlight.

Make sure your surface is uncluttered. It can be a table, a desk, or a shelf in a closet. Keep a stack of newspapers nearby to cover your workspace and make it easy to clean up afterwards. Remember that most projects take time to dry and may need to sit—so the area you choose should not have a lot of traffic. *Translation:* Avoid using the dining room table if that's where your family eats their meals.

Finally, be near a source of water and an adequate power supply. No craft room should be without a good extension cord or power strip. Buy a quality one from the hardware store, and be careful not to overload it. Setting up your craft area near a sink for easy cleanup is great, but not always possible. Keep a jug of water and a household bucket nearby.

This is an actual photo of my craft table. Believe it or not, for me, this is organized!

What You Need

The following is a list of supplies to keep on hand. This is just a guide. Each project in this book is complete with a list of materials needed. It would be best to have all the materials on the list before you begin the project, so check your craft closet first. And if you are unable to find what you need at your local craft store, refer to our resource guide (Best Places for Craft Supplies, page 204).

BASIC TOOLS
awl, a pointed tool
hammer
hole punch
hot-glue gun
iron and ironing board
measuring tape
ruler
scissors
staple gun
stapler
wire cutters
X-Acto knife

GROWN-UPS: There is nothing worse than trying to cut fabric with scissors that "bend" the material instead of making a precise, clean cut. Cutting cardboard, pipe cleaners, and even paper can make scissors dull. It is best to keep a pair of scissors marked *paper scissors* in your craft supplies. To sharpen a pair of scissors: Cut a piece of sandpaper into strips, using long, even cuts.

CRAFT SUPPLIES
acrylic craft paints
assorted paintbrushes
balloons
craft wire
crayons
glue (fabric, glue sticks, paper, tacky, white craft, and wood)
glitter
Mod Podge (gloss and matte)
pencils, pens, and markers
pipe cleaners (chenille stems)
sandpaper
spray adhesive
spray paint
tape (cellophane, duct, electrical, and masking)
tempera paint
tissue paper
wire
wooden Popsicle sticks

HOUSEHOLD SUPPLIES
aluminum foil
buckets
clothespins
dishtowels and rags
gallon jug, with water
paper towels
plastic cups and plates
plastic freezer bags
sponges (compressed, kitchen, and sea)
string
toothpicks

PAPER SUPPLIES
construction paper
graph paper
kraft paper
patterned paper
tracing paper
waxed paper

SEWING SUPPLIES
dressmaker's chalk
iron-on adhesive
pins (safety, straight, and t-pins)
sewing needles

THINGS TO COLLECT, SAVE, AND RECYCLE
beads and gems
buttons (all sizes and colors)
cans and small bottles
leaves
magazines
newspaper
nonreturnable bottles
paper towel rolls
ribbons
scrap fabric
seashells
stamps
stickers
wrapping paper

Be Prepared

SAFETY FIRST
Crafting is fun, but it can be dangerous too. Many household items can be harmful if mixed together or used improperly. The craft projects in our book should be supervised by a grown-up. Take the time to read the labels on all the items you are using—before you use them. Always follow the manufacturer's instructions closely: Using the directions will not only keep you and your family safe, but it will also set a good example for your children.

DOUBLE-CHECK YOUR MEASUREMENTS
Always measure twice before you pick up those scissors. You will not be able to undo a cut if you make a mistake.

KNOW YOUR GLUES
Most craft projects use regular white craft glue, which is washable, dries quickly, and glues paper, wood, cloth, and more. But you should also be aware of the wide variety of glues created for different mediums. Fabric glue is formulated to use on cloth and is permanent, so it will not wash out. Paper glue will not shrink or saturate, which is what causes ripples in paper. Mod Podge is a multipurpose glue that dries clear, so you can use it to seal or add a smooth finish to a project. Tacky glue is extra thick and dries clear, so it works well on projects involving wood, metal, glass, ceramics, and most plastics. Adhesive sprays and hot-glue guns require adult supervision, so it's important to read the instructions and manufacturer's suggestions about ventilation and uses.

...AND YOUR PAINTS
The last thing you want to do is use the wrong paint. Here's a quick primer: The best paint for paper or cardboard is tempera paint. Acrylic paint works best on wood, clay, metal, and plastic because of its thickness. When working with fabric, be sure to use fabric paint that's formulated so that it will not crack or wash out.

A Note About Saving the Planet

Be careful what you toss in the trash. Some common household items can be great storage containers for the supplies in your craft room. Egg cartons, old ice trays, and baby-food jars become places to keep beads and buttons. Shoeboxes make excellent storage for glue sticks and crayons, and coffee cans are perfect for holding brushes and pencils.

Another way you can recycle these household items is to make the craft projects in this book. Why not turn a jam jar into a Glitter Globe or a giant cardboard box into our Peekaboo Puppet Theater? Keep broken china to add to a Baubles & Beads Mosaic Pot and bits of old crayons to turn into a beautiful Sun Catcher Mobile on an afternoon when it's pouring outside and everyone is stir-crazy. This is a fun lesson in eco-awareness for your kids—and a smart way to utilize what you already have in a meaningful way.

FYI
Here is a key to the abbreviations used in **CRAFTY U**:

c = cup
in. = inch
lb. = pound
oz. = ounce
qt. = quart
t = teaspoon
T = tablespoon
yd. = yard

Every day is a DECOUPAGE DAY

Cuff Love

Decoupage an armful of these bright bracelets with stripes, circles, or any pattern you like. Cut the cardboard ahead of time, and have a stack of colorful tissue paper and a couple of pots of glue on hand.

WHAT YOU NEED

cardboard tube (one left over from
    wrapping paper or a mailing tube)
scissors
white craft paint
small paintbrushes
colored tissue paper
Mod Podge glue

HOW TO MAKE

1. Cut the cardboard tube into 1½-in. or 2-in. widths or to whatever size bracelet you want. Paint the pieces with the white paint as a base coat. Let dry.

2. Cut or tear light-colored tissue paper into pieces. Using a paintbrush, apply a thin layer of glue to the bracelet and apply tissue paper. For deeper color, add more layers of glue and tissue until you get the desired base color.

3. Cut shapes out of a darker shade of tissue paper and apply to the base layer with glue. Paint a coat of glue on the finished bracelet. Let dry.

Black & White & Read All Over

Decoupage is one of the easiest crafts to do—and one of the most enjoyable. We took an unfinished chest of drawers, a Chinese newspaper, and a pot of glue and made something wonderful.

WHAT YOU NEED

scissors
Chinese newspaper, or any interesting
   newsprint, like the funny pages
   of your local paper
paintbrush
Mod Podge glue
small chest of drawers

HOW TO MAKE

1. Plan your design: We used small and large type to make a simple statement with bold borders, but you can also work with photos or ads in the newspaper to create visual excitement. Cut out squares and rectangles in different sizes. Apply a thin layer of glue to the back of each newspaper piece, then lay each piece on chest and smooth in place with the paintbrush (don't worry if pieces overlap). Completely cover chest with newspaper.

2. For a smooth finish, apply two coats of glue to entire chest. Let dry 1 hour between coats; allow chest to dry overnight before use.

If your town doesn't have a Chinese market, you can download a Chinese newspaper off the Web (www.onlinenewspapers.com).

Take a Snapshot Tray

With a bit of ingenuity, you can use your favorite photographs to create a great present for Mom, Dad, Grandma, or Grandpa. It's a gift that will be neat to look at every time it's used.

WHAT YOU NEED

sandpaper
large wooden tray
acrylic craft paint
medium paintbrushes
scissors
color copies of your photos
   in various sizes
construction paper
Mod Podge glue

HOW TO MAKE

1. Lightly sand the tray and cover with one or two coats of paint.

2. Trim your photos to a variety of sizes, and create any other construction paper artwork desired.

3. Arrange the photos and artwork in interesting ways on the tray, overlapping the edges or placing photos at different angles. Once you like the design, glue pieces to the tray. Once dry, paint another coat or two of glue over the finished tray. Let dry.

HAppy
Mother's
DAY!

Light Up Your Life Switch Plates

Here is a cool project: Decoupage a simple light-switch cover with bold and colorful stamps or bubble gum wrappers. Feel free to improvise—a favorite comic strip could work too!

WHAT YOU NEED

> white light-switch plates
> candy or bubble gum wrappers
> stamps
> iron and ironing board
> paper towels
> Mod Podge glue
> small paintbrush
> scissors

HOW TO MAKE

1. Flatten out the wrappers. GROWN-UPS: Place wrappers between two paper towels and iron them at a low temperature to smooth them out. You can also use color copies of them instead.

2. Apply candy wrappers or stamps to the switch plate with glue. Line up the wrappers to make a graphic pattern, or overlap stamps in a more random way. Trim away any excess along the edges. Paint an additional coat of glue over the entire switch plate. Let dry.

JUMP UP! it's SPRING

Cheep-Cheep Chicks

With a few snips of the scissors, you and your kids can create these cutie-patootie creatures from bright paper, wire, glue, and beads in about half an hour.

WHAT YOU NEED

- yellow crepe paper
- scissors
- thin wire
- thick craft glue
- orange tissue paper
- small black beads

HOW TO MAKE

1. Cut four 3 x 4 in. rectangles out of a sheet of crepe paper. Stack and fold the rectangles accordion-style.

2. Take a small piece of wire and wrap it tightly around the middle of the stack.

3. To make the chick's fluffy feathers, pull each layer toward the wire, to form a pom-pom.

4. Repeat Steps 1 through 3 with four 2 x 3-in. pieces of crepe paper for the chick's head.

5. Use a dot of thick craft glue to attach the chick's head to the chick's body.

6. For the beak, cut a piece of orange tissue paper into a ½-in. square. Fold it in half diagonally to create a triangle. Put a dab of glue on the folded edge and position the beak on the chick's head.

7. Put a drop of glue on the 2 black beads and glue eyes to chick's head.

8. A creative way to use your chick: Glue it onto a paper cup or eggcup and fill the cup with Easter candy.

Paper Petal Blooms

Spring comes early at your house when you and your kids transform tissue paper and pipe cleaners into these easy, petal-perfect blossoms.

WHAT YOU NEED

coffee cup
pencil
colorful tissue paper
scissors
pipe cleaners

HOW TO MAKE

1. Using a coffee cup approximately 4 in. in diameter as a template, trace circles onto the tissue paper. For each flower, cut 9 circles out of tissue to create the petals.

2. Use the end of a pipe cleaner to poke a hole in the middle of the tissue paper circles. Slide the circles up the pipe cleaner and twist each end of the pipe cleaner to hold the petals in place.

3. One by one, fold the circles up and gently adjust each one to look like a petal.

I Want Candy Napkin Rings

These adorable rings make the table look cheerful and are a cinch to make from narrow plastic tubing. Plus, everyone can wear them home!

WHAT YOU NEED

plastic tubing in ⅜-in. diameter
   (from hardware store)
scissors
tiny colorful candy that will fit
   into the narrow tubing
chopstick or bamboo skewer (optional)
plastic tubing in ½-in. diameter

HOW TO MAKE

1. For 1 ring: Cut a 6-in. piece of the narrower, ⅜-in. tubing for a napkin ring.

2. Fill the tube with candy. If any pieces get stuck, use a chopstick or bamboo skewer to push candies through the tube.

3. Cut a 1-in. piece of the wider tubing. Use that piece to connect the ends of the napkin ring by sliding both ends of the narrower tubing into the wider tubing.

Super-Duper Eggs

Anything goes when it comes to decorating Easter eggs: Use polka dots, stripes, daisies, letter cutouts, and star stickers to brighten them up. Encourage kids to get creative when picking colors.

WHAT YOU NEED

dozen hard-boiled eggs
egg-dye kit
bowls
drafting or masking tape or contact paper
hole punch
assorted stickers
straight pins
tongs or slotted spoon
colorful pipe cleaners

HOW TO MAKE

1. For the base color: Prepare bowls of egg dye, following directions on the egg-dye kit. Dip each egg into dye; let it sit until it's the color you want. Remove the egg from the dye and let dry.

2. You can create patterns on the eggshell by using some tape and a different color dye. Apply narrow strips of tape to create stripes; use a hole punch to make polka dots and stick them on the shell; you can also use cutouts, or star or letter stickers. Once you've applied the tape or stickers, dip the egg into another, darker color, then take it out and let it dry. Carefully remove tape or contact paper cutouts to see your design.

3. Try a variation: Apply tape, stickers, or contact paper to a dry white egg. Dip the egg into dye, then remove and let dry. Carefully remove the applications and reveal the white pattern left behind.

For hollow eggs

1. If you plan on decorating eggs to hang on an Easter egg tree, you need to blow out the insides of the eggs before decorating. Working over an empty bowl, use a straight pin to poke a small hole in the narrow end of the egg and a large hole at the wide end; break the yolk with the pin. Blow out the inside of the egg through the larger hole into the bowl. You might want to use an egg-blowing tool (available at craft stores). Rinse the egg out with water.

2. Carefully dip the eggshells in boiling water to kill any bacteria, use tongs or a slotted spoon to get them out, and then allow to dry.

3. Decorate following Steps 1 through 3, handling eggshells with care so they don't break.

4. Thread a pipe cleaner through both holes, creating a loop at the top so you can hang the egg. Adjust pipe cleaner so egg won't slip off.

Crazy Carrot Party Bags

Think of them as Easter stockings and fill these larger-than-life bags with lots of treats. Allot plenty of time for this project, which involves cutting and sewing.

WHAT YOU NEED

For 1 bag

	chalk for marking
1½ yds.	orange felt
	scissors
	straight pins and needle
	orange and green embroidery floss
¾ yd.	green felt
¾ yd.	ribbon

HOW TO MAKE

1. Enlarge the carrot template on page 200, so the top of the orange part of the carrot measures about 8 in. and the length is about 19 in.

2. Place the template on the orange felt and use chalk to trace the orange part of the carrot. Cut out two carrot shapes and put one aside for the back. For the front of the carrot: Cut horizontally on the line indicated on the template, about one-third of the way down from the top, so that you end up with 2 pieces.

3. Pin the two front pieces on top of the single back piece. Using the needle and orange floss, stitch all around the outside edges of the carrot. Leave open the front panel where it's been cut to create a deep pocket for treats.

4. For decoration, use the needle and orange embroidery floss to stitch horizontal lines across the two front pieces of the carrot.

5. Use the chalk to trace the carrot-top portion of the template on the green felt. Cut out 2 carrot tops: Pin 1 to the top of each side of the carrot. Stitch around the edges of the carrot top with the needle and green embroidery floss. Also stitch through the 4 layers of fabric at the base of the carrot top.

6. Cut the ribbon in half and sew the ends of the ribbon to the back of the carrot. Tie carrot to chair before filling the pocket with wrapped candies or toys.

A-tisket, A-tasket Basket

Use colorful paper, a hole punch, and pretty ribbon to weave the sides together. Tuck surprises inside (foil-wrapped candies, decorated Easter eggs, and a yummy white chocolate bunny) and top it with a paper petal bloom.

WHAT YOU NEED

pen for tracing
scissors
heavy stock or corrugated paper
hole punch
narrow ribbon

HOW TO MAKE

1. Enlarge the basket template on page 201 to make the basket size you want. Trace the template onto the underside of stock paper or the smooth side of the corrugated paper. Cut out the template.

2. Form the box by folding the sides up on the dotted lines. Punch holes at the marked circles.

3. The box is held together with ribbon: Cut a piece of ribbon that is twice the height of the folded box. Start at one corner of the box and pull one end of the ribbon through the two bottom holes to the outside of the box so there are two equal lengths of ribbon.

4. Lace one end of the ribbon through the next hole on the opposite side. Do the same with the other end of the ribbon. Continue to lace the ribbon till you get to the top holes, then tie the ribbon in a knot. Repeat at each corner until basket is laced up.

5. For the handle, cut a strip of paper about 2 to 3 in. wide that is in proportion to the size of your basket. Punch two holes on both ends of the handle, and on two opposite sides of the basket.

6. Place handle inside the basket and line up the holes of the handle and basket. Thread ribbon through the holes on one end of the handle and one side of the box; tie to secure. Repeat for the other set of holes.

7. Attach a Paper Petal Bloom (see page 34) and let the kids affix stickers or cutouts.

Hippity Hop
Bunny Piñata

Start this easy-to-make piñata a few days before you need it to allow the papier-mâché to dry completely. Filled with Easter goodies, this adorable swinger is sure to delight all your funny little bunnies from start to finish.

WHAT YOU NEED

flour
water
plastic bucket
large round balloon
newspaper torn into 3 x 5-in. strips
string
clothesline
straight pin
cardboard or poster board
masking tape
sponge brush
white craft paint
white glue
white confetti
2 small brown pom-poms
large yellow pom-pom
green pipe cleaner
utility knife

HOW TO MAKE

1. Mix 2 c flour with 2 c water in plastic bucket to make a thick papier-mâché paste.

2. Blow up the balloon and tie a knot on the top. Take strips of newspaper and dip into the papier-mâché paste; apply one at a time to the balloon, overlapping pieces, and covering it completely with 3 to 4 layers. Cut a 2-in. length of string and tie to the knot on the balloon. Hang it on the clothesline to dry for a day or two.

3. When piñata is completely dry, pop the balloon with a straight pin.

4. Cut the cardboard or poster board into bunny ears (make each about 12 in. long) and attach to the top of the head with masking tape. Cover with more papier-mâché. Let dry.

5. Apply another coat of papier-mâché, especially around the ears, and let dry.

6. Use sponge brush and white craft paint to paint the whole piñata white—you may have to do 2 coats for it to look uniform.

7. When the paint is dry, use sponge brush to "paint" the piñata with white glue. Pour white confetti onto a layer of newspaper, and roll the piñata over the confetti so the surface is covered.

8. When the piñata is dry, use a dab of glue to add the brown pom-pom eyes and yellow pom-pom nose. Cut the green pipe cleaner in half for whiskers; glue under nose.

9. Cut a small slot or hole with a utility knife in the back of the piñata and fill with wrapped candies and/or toys. Seal the opening with tape.

Heidi's Yummy Easter Eggs

Rosie's sister-in-law Heidi created these cool-looking edible eggs from eggshells filled with colored chocolates. GROWN-UPS: This project takes some prep work to get the shells ready, but kids get a kick out of creating the layers.

WHAT YOU NEED

1 dozen eggs (keep the carton handy)
bowl
straight pin
tongs or slotted spoon
masking or plastic tape
microwave-safe cup
Wilton Candy Melts chocolates in assorted colors and milk, dark, and white chocolate (available at craft stores or www.wilton.com)
quart-size resealable freezer bags
scissors
cake frosting
colorful candies

HOW TO MAKE

1. Blow out the insides of the eggs: Working over an empty bowl, use a straight pin to poke a small hole in the narrow end of the egg and a large hole at the wide end; break the yolk with the pin. Blow out the inside of the egg through the larger hole into the bowl. You might want to use an egg-blowing tool (available at craft stores). Rinse the egg out with water.

2. Carefully dip the eggshells in boiling water to kill any bacteria, use tongs or a slotted spoon to get them out, and then allow to dry.

3. Once the eggshells are dry, put a piece of tape over the small end. Smooth tape out so there are no wrinkles.

4. Place in egg carton; repeat Steps 1 through 3 with as many eggs as you want to make.

5. Put one color of Wilton Candy Melts in a microwave-safe cup. Melt the chocolate 30 seconds at a time, stirring each time. Once it's melted, but not hot, scoop into a quart-size freezer bag. Note: Be careful not to get a drop of water in the chocolate or it will harden.

6. You're ready to begin filling the empty eggshells. Poke a small hole in a corner of the freezer bag, just big enough so that you can control the flow of chocolate. Fill the eggs with a few teaspoons of one color, then melt another color and repeat. Continue to layer chocolates any way you choose.

7. Once an egg is filled to the top, tap it a little to make sure all of the air gets out and the chocolate settles. Place egg (open end up) back in the egg carton. Put carton in the refrigerator overnight.

8. Remove eggs from the refrigerator. Take out an egg and tap it lightly on the counter, then peel it like a boiled egg. For a final touch, use a dab of frosting as glue to affix a colorful candy to the top of each egg.

To Mom, with Love Bouquet

These adorable paper blossoms are a cinch to make. Cut out the flowers and show your kids how to construct one, and then let them put together a big bunch. Practice your look of amazement for the moment they give the bouquet to you. (*Wow* and *cool* are always good words to use.)

WHAT YOU NEED

    pencil
    flower-shaped cookie cutters
      (2 different sizes)
    colorful construction paper
    scissors
    round hole punch
20 colorful 12-in. pipe cleaners
40 plastic beads

HOW TO MAKE

1. Use a pencil to trace 40 cookie cutter flower shapes on construction paper (20 small and 20 large). Cut out.

2. For each blossom, put a small flower on top of a large flower; punch 2 holes in center, ½ in. apart. Loop pipe cleaner up through 1 hole, slide on 2 beads, bend pipe cleaner down, and loop it through other hole. Twist pipe cleaner ends together to create stem. Twenty stems will make a beautiful bouquet.

You Big Sweetie Cupcakes

What could be more delectable than a bouquet of cupcakes! Share the sweetness of Mother's Day with family and friends by bringing this yummy centerpiece to your big celebration.

WHAT YOU NEED

For cupcakes

7   cupcakes with white frosting in
        paper cupcake liners
1 bag multicolored Starburst Fruit Chews
        waxed paper
        rolling pin
        flower-shaped cookie cutters
           (2 different flower shapes)
        colorful cereal, jelly beans, or gumdrops

For flowerpot

        6-in. clay flowerpot
        paper towels
        acrylic craft paint in two colors
        paintbrushes
        floral foam to fit inside flowerpot
           (to about 1 in. from top of pot)
        scissors
7   bamboo skewers
        colorful shredded paper

HOW TO MAKE

1. To make a flower, unwrap 3 same-color candies and line them up side-by-side between 2 sheets of waxed paper. Using a rolling pin, roll candies out until you have a circle large enough to cut out 1 flower with cookie cutter. Repeat until you have 7 flowers.

2. Put 1 flower on top of each cupcake. Using a dab of frosting as glue, stick a piece of cereal, jellybean, or gumdrop on top of each flower. Set cupcakes aside.

3. Wash and dry flowerpot thoroughly. Put flowerpot on paper towels and use 1 color of acrylic paint to cover outer surface; let dry. Paint a design with the other color; let dry.

4. Put floral foam inside pot. Trim dull end of bamboo skewers with scissors so each is about 1 in. longer than the pot is tall. Insert skewers (trimmed ends first) into floral foam, placing 1 in center and the others in a circle around it. Push 1 cupcake onto each skewer, until the cupcake rests on floral foam.

5. Gently stuff the shredded paper into the spaces between the cupcakes, leaving some of the paper hanging over the edges.

All About You Frames

Spiff up a simple wooden frame as a surprise gift for Dad's big day. You can use almost anything to cover it—fabrics such as pinstriped cotton or gray flannel, or a map of a favorite city or vacation spot.

WHAT YOU NEED

wooden frame
shirting, suit fabric, or maps (cut to size to overlap frame by 2 to 4 in.)
spray adhesive
fabric glue (for cloth-covered frame)
Mod Podge glue (for map-covered frame)
white chalk
X-Acto knife
scissors
clip-on bow tie, buttons, or small souvenirs

HOW TO MAKE

1. GROWN-UPS: Take out the cardboard backing and piece of glass from the frame to work with the wooden part only.

2. Put fabric or map right side down on table. Lightly coat front of your frame with spray adhesive. Press the frame, sticky side down, onto fabric or map.

3. Wrap fabric or map around the back of frame, neatly smoothing wrinkles or bumps on front. Glue into place using fabric glue (for the cloth-covered frame) or Mod Podge glue (for the map-covered frame), one section at a time, folding and smoothing any excess into place. Let dry.

4. To make the frame opening, use chalk to draw a rectangle that's about 2 in. from all four inside edges. Use X-Acto knife to cut an X inside the rectangle, then trim the excess fabric or map, cutting along the chalk line with scissors. Apply glue onto inside edge of frame; fold fabric or map over the frame and press into place.

5. For cloth-covered frame, use fabric glue to affix bow tie and buttons to front of frame. Let dry.

6. For a smooth finish on the map-covered frame, apply two coats of Mod Podge glue over the entire surface. Let dry 1 hour between coats. Glue on small toys or souvenirs to remind you of a recent road trip or getaway.

Meet My Peeps Bird Feeder

Inspire young bird lovers with this bright sunflower feeder. Save up pet-food or tuna-fish cans for kids to paint yellow and brown. Assemble it outside in your garden—and watch the birds show up for lunch!

WHAT YOU NEED

    paintbrush
    clean pet-food or tuna-fish cans
       (1 large, 7 small)
    metal paint (brown and yellow)
    metal flower fence ornament
       (available at www.homegoods.com)
    sponge
    heavy-duty self-adhesive Velcro
    hammer
    nail
    bailing wire
    wire cutters
    birdseed

HOW TO MAKE

1. Paint large can brown and small cans and metal flower ornament yellow. Let dry; repeat with a second coat. Let dry.

2. Dip sponge into brown paint and blot excess. Use sponge to paint the center of the metal ornament so that it resembles the center of a sunflower. Let dry.

3. Stick Velcro pieces on the bottoms of the cans and the places on the sunflower where the cans will sit. Attach large can to the center of the sunflower and 1 small can to each petal.

4. For hanging wires, make 3 holes around the middle can in a triangle formation. (If it is a 6-petal flower ornament like the one we used, you would make a hole in every other petal.) How to do it: Hammer a nail through the metal ornament; remove nail. Cut 3 1-yd. lengths of wire; insert each length through each hole. Secure wire by twisting ends below the feeder.

5. Bring the wire ends together above the feeder and make a loop. Cut a 12-in. length of wire and wrap it around the loop.

6. Hang the feeder on your favorite tree and fill the cans with birdseed.

Chillin' on a Summer Day

BLOOM'S DAY
- Pretty as a Posy Pencil Holders
- Green Gallery Flower Prints
- Just for You Plates
- Yes, You Can Cans

ARTS & CRAFTS TIME!
- Beads of Wonder
- Friends Forever Bracelets
- Way-Cool Painted Sneakers
- Rainbow Wraps
- To Tie-Dye-For T-Shirts
- Chalk It Up

FOURTH OF JULY
- Party Pinwheels

FROM THE SEA
- Super Star Shells
- Glam Clam Paperweight & Starring You Frame
- Royal (Icing) Sand Castle
- Ocean in a Jar
- By the Sea Sand Art

Pretty as a Posy Pencil Holders

Make an imprint of a flower or leaf using this easy-to-master technique, which involves lightly pounding petals or leaves onto fabric or paper. These impressions can be used in many ways—to wrap around a can for a pencil holder or to display as a botanical gallery.

WHAT YOU NEED

- fabric or paper (printed or watercolor paper looks pretty too)
- scissors
- leaves
- flowers (preferably ones with just one layer of petals, like daisies)
- cellophane tape
- wooden board
- paper towels
- rubber mallet or hammer
- tin cans
- craft glue
- ribbons
- colored construction paper

HOW TO MAKE

1. Cut a piece of fabric or paper to fit around a clean, label-free tin can.

2. Cut the stems off the flowers you've chosen.

3. Lay a leaf or flower facedown on the fabric or paper. Hold it in place with tape, if needed.

4. Put the wooden board on a hard surface. Lay the taped leaf or flower between 2 paper towels on top of the wooden board.

5. GROWN-UPS: Please help your kids with this step. Hold the paper towels in place and pound the paper towel with the rubber mallet or hammer in the spot over the leaf or flower. No need to rush: Take your time, don't pound too hard, and always make sure your fingers are out of the way of the rubber mallet or hammer.

6. Once you're done, carefully pull back the top towel and remove the tape and the leaf or flower.

7. Apply craft glue to the edges of the paper or fabric and wrap around the can. Let dry. Cut two pieces of ribbon to fit the top and bottom of the can; glue trim in place.

Green Gallery Flower Prints

Keep a favorite blossom or graceful fern forever by making an imprint of it using an easy technique: You gently pound the petals or leaves to make a lasting impression on fabric or paper. The results are beautiful enough to frame!

WHAT YOU NEED

fabric or paper (printed or watercolor
   paper looks pretty too)
scissors
leaves
flowers (preferably ones with just
   one layer of petals, like daisies)
cellophane tape
wooden board
paper towels
rubber mallet or hammer
colored construction paper
picture frames with mats

HOW TO MAKE

1. When making a print to frame, choose paper or fabric that's slightly smaller than the opening of your mat, leaving room for a colorful 1- to 2-in. border.

2. Cut the stems off the flowers you've chosen.

3. Lay a leaf or flower facedown on the fabric or paper. Hold it in place with tape, if needed.

4. Put the wooden board on a hard surface. Lay the taped leaf or flower and fabric between 2 paper towels on top of the wooden board.

5. GROWN-UPS: Please help your kids with this step. Hold the paper towels in place and pound the paper towel with the rubber mallet or hammer. No need to rush: Take your time, don't pound too hard, and always make sure your fingers are out of the way of the rubber mallet or hammer.

6. Once you're done, carefully pull back the top towel and remove the tape and the leaf or flower.

7. Before framing your pounded leaf or flower impression, cut colorful construction paper to fit the opening of the frame. Glue the paper or fabric with the impression in the center of the construction paper, leaving a 1- to 2-in. border. Place inside the matted picture frame.

Just for You Plates

Pick a favorite piece of artwork and create a decoupage gift for Mom or a good friend. All that's needed is a pot of glue, pretty tissue paper, and a clear glass plate. Great results and big smiles are guaranteed!

WHAT YOU NEED

- kid's artwork
- clear glass plate
- white paper
- pencil
- scissors or decorative-edge scissors
- printed or solid tissue paper
- foam paintbrush
- Mod Podge glue
- permanent marker

HOW TO MAKE

1. Rather than working with the original, you should make a few photocopies of the artwork for your collage so you feel free to experiment with your design.

2. Lay the plate facedown and trace around it on the piece of white paper. Add a 1½-in. border around the edges.

3. Think about how you want your plate to look and sketch out a rough design. Use scissors or decorative-edge scissors to cut out the photocopied artwork to place in the center of the paper circle. Write messages or phrases on small pieces of paper, then arrange them with pieces of tissue paper around the artwork.

4. Once you've laid out your collage, use the foam paintbrush to apply a light layer of glue to the front of the artwork. Starting at the center, lay the artwork on the back of the plate and smooth out any bubbles. Apply the remaining pieces of the collage with glue. Tip: Cut slits in the paper to make it easier to smooth it flat on the curved edges of the plate.

5. Let the plate dry, then clean up edges of the plate by cutting off any excess paper.

6. Cover the collage on the back of the plate with a layer of glue and a layer of the tissue paper. Let dry; apply a few more coats of glue. Clean up edges of the plate by cutting off any excess tissue paper.

7. Make sure to add your name and the date with a permanent marker on the back of your plate. You might want to hang it up on the wall using a plate hanger. And remember that it's decorative and should never be washed. Wipe it clean with a soft towel or paper cloth.

Yes, You Can Cans

Colorful paint and cool trims transform tossables into a pencil holder, a vase for daisies, or a place to stash craft pens. GROWN-UPS: Teach kids about the joy of recycling an old, clean can into a bright and shiny new thing!

WHAT YOU NEED

foam paintbrushes
acrylic craft paints
clean tin cans with labels removed
artist paintbrushes
craft glue
colorful paper trims

HOW TO MAKE

1. Paint outside of cans using foam brush and craft paint. Let dry.

2. Paint bands of color around the cans using the foam paintbrush and craft paints.

3. Paint stripes, polka dots, pretty flowers, squiggles, or anything you like on cans using an artist paintbrush for detailing. Let dry.

4. Apply colorful paper trim with glue along the top and bottom of the can.

ARTS & CRAFTS TIME!

Set up a table with colorful supplies and get kids going on fun projects to wear (cute beads, tie-dye tees) and share (bright braids, friendship bracelets).

Beads of Wonder

Everyone likes creating these sunny little baubles. Each bead is unique—and you can design as many or as few of them as you want on your necklace. GROWN-UPS: This simple project requires your supervision because the clay beads need to bake in the oven.

WHAT YOU NEED

Fimo or Sculpey clay (available at
   art-supply and craft stores)
metal skewer
narrow twine or silk cord

HOW TO MAKE

1. Take a small piece of clay and roll it between your hands into a bead. Make the number of beads you want for your necklace (we made between 15 and 20) and then decorate them. If you want dots or bands, take tiny balls or rolled-up strips of clay and apply them to a bead and roll it gently between your hands to smooth the details in.

2. With a skewer, carefully poke holes through the centers of the beads.

3. With a little help from a grown-up, bake the clay according to the package directions. Be sure to let the beads cool completely before starting Step 4.

4. Using twine or silk cord, string your beads. Your Beads of Wonder are now ready to wear!

Friends Forever Bracelets

Follow the diagrams using just two colors until you get the hang of it. Start by making a narrow bracelet, then double the amount of embroidery thread to make a thicker one. Other materials that will yield cool results are silk cording or lanyard.

WHAT YOU NEED

2 25-in.-long strands of embroidery thread in two of your favorite colors
tape
colorful beads

HOW TO MAKE

1 Fold strands in half, then knot the strands together about 1½ in. from the top.

2 Tape the top loop to a table or cutting board; separate strands by color (fig. a).

3 Braid the strands by following the diagrams shown (fig. b, c, and d), pulling strands tightly as you go (fig. e).

4 Repeat sequence; slip beads on wherever you want as you go.

5 Tie ends together with a knot to make a bracelet.

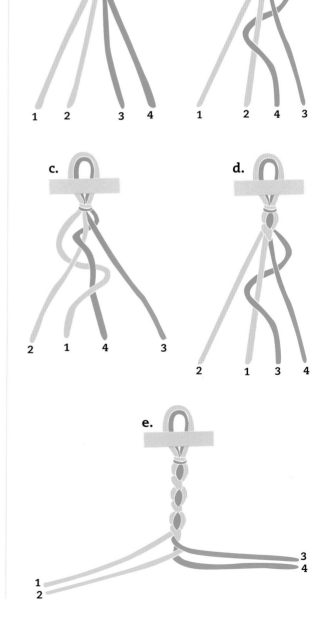

Way-Cool Painted Sneakers

Can you believe how crazy-expensive customized sneakers are? These shoes give kids a chance to show off their skills at painting something creative and kooky that they'll slip on and kick off all summer long.

WHAT YOU NEED

newspaper
clean canvas sneakers
fabric or acrylic craft paint
artist paintbrushes
fabric paint pens

HOW TO MAKE

1 Cover a work surface with newspaper.

2 Using fabric paints and paint pens, decorate sneakers.

3 Let fabric paint dry for 24 hours before painting another shade on top of the original color.

Rainbow Wraps

Ooh la la! How exciting is it to do each other's hair and make it look like you just got back from the Caribbean? This is an activity that can be done anywhere—at the beach or in your own backyard. Set up a basket of colorful embroidery thread and teach your sweeties how to braid.

WHAT YOU NEED

    tiny rubber bands
    colorful embroidery thread
    scissors
    mini hair clip

HOW TO MAKE

For a wrapped braid

1. On the side of your head, make a skinny braid. Tie it at the end with a rubber band.

2. Cut three or four 10-in.-long pieces of embroidery thread in different colors. For our braids, we used four colors: fuchsia, turquoise, black, and yellow.

3. Take one piece of embroidery thread, and knot it tightly at the top of your braid, about ½ in. from the scalp. Take the thread and wrap it tightly around the braid, for 1 or 2 in., leaving about 1 in. of the thread at the bottom. Use a hair clip to hold the end flat against the braid while you knot and wrap a second color over the loose end of the first and continue for an inch or two.

4. Repeat with other colors. After the entire braid is wrapped, knot the end of the last thread around the braid. Snip excess embroidery thread.

For a colorful woven braid

1. On the side of your head, make a skinny pigtail. Tie it with a rubber band about ½ in. from your scalp.

2. Cut 6 long pieces of colorful embroidery thread; each piece should be double the length of the pigtail. Holding the pieces together, fold them in half.

3. Cover up the rubber band, placing the middle of the "fold" on top of the band and tying the pieces in a knot underneath the skinny pigtail.

4. Separate the embroidery threads into 2 sections; your hair will be the third.

5. Now, braid the sections together. Use another rubber band to secure the sections at the bottom. Cut off excess embroidery thread.

To Tie-Dye-For T-Shirts

How neat are these! You can give a favorite old comfy T-shirt a brand-new cool look and teach kids how to do tie-dye. **GROWN-UPS: Have plenty of plastic gloves on hand, so no one ends up with blue hands.**

WHAT YOU NEED

white cotton T-shirt
12 rubber bands
fabric dye
plastic squirt bottle for each dye color
disposable latex gloves
bucket or large bowl

HOW TO MAKE

1. If you are using a new T-shirt, make sure you wash it first. Sometimes fabrics are treated with sizing or starches that will resist dye.

2. Pinch a small piece of the T-shirt and secure it with a rubber band.

3. Gather up more of the T-shirt and bind it with another rubber band an inch or so away from the first rubber band. Repeat all over the T-shirt. (See next page for alternative tie-dye techniques.)

4. When working with dye, always wear gloves. Mix dye according to manufacturer's directions, then siphon each color into its own plastic squirt bottle.

5. Place T-shirt in bucket or bowl. Squirt dye colors wherever you want on the T-shirt. Use as many colors as desired, covering the entire shirt with dye. Let it soak for about 20 minutes.

6. Rinse the T-shirt with cold water until the water runs clear.

7. Remove the rubber bands. Sometimes the shirt will stretch out in places; you can fix this by drying it in the dryer. Remember to wash dyed items separately for the first few times, as dyes have a tendency to run.

Follow Step 1 (on the previous page), then substitute one of these other cool techniques for Steps 2 and 3 for unique tie-dye patterns.

Big Circles

Tie rubber bands around fabric, spacing the bands as close or as far as you want.

Circles

Before dyeing, tie Ping Pong balls, plastic Wiffle balls, marbles, small rubber balls, stones, holiday ornaments, shells, or other round items in the fabric.

Stripes

Pleat your T-shirt, from side to side, and then tie it at intervals as shown.

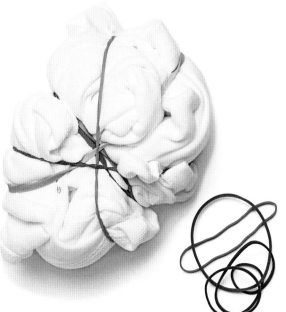

Spirals

Pinch the fabric where you want the center of the spiral to be. Spin the fabric clockwise to make a tight bundle. Wrap rubber bands around the outside of the bundle before dyeing.

Chalk It Up

Mix up a big batch of chalk in whatever colors you want! This recipe calls for simple ingredients with results that are simply spectacular.

WHAT YOU NEED

For one piece of chalk

1 c warm water
2 c plaster of paris
    mixing bowl
    spoon
    powdered tempera paint
    toilet paper tube
    plastic wrap
    masking tape or rubber band
    waxed paper

HOW TO MAKE

1. Pour the warm water into the mixing bowl. Sprinkle the plaster of paris into the water while stirring with the spoon. Add just a little at a time, until it is thoroughly mixed.

2. Mix in the tempera paint (1 T at a time) until you reach the desired intensity of color.

3. Cover one end of toilet paper tube with plastic wrap, and hold it in place with tape or a rubber band. Make a liner with the waxed paper, and slip it inside the tube to keep the plaster of paris from sticking.

4. Pour the plaster mixture into tube. Tap the side of the tube to release any air bubbles. Set aside and let dry for 24 to 48 hours. Gently remove chalk.

5. Repeat Steps 1 to 4 using other paint colors. Be careful when you clean up, as plaster of paris can clog your sink. It is best to clean up the mixing bowl in a larger bucket of water (to dissolve and dilute the plaster). You can also do it outside with a garden hose.

Party Pinwheels

Your motto? Anything goes! These patriotic decorations are simple and bright, but feel free to show your independence and make them out of a sheet of graphic gift wrap or paper that kids have scribbled on with crayons.

WHAT YOU NEED

scissors
red, white, and blue patterned papers
stapler
hole punch
string or ribbon

HOW TO MAKE

1. Cut the paper into squares in big and small sizes.

2. Take one square and start by making a 1-in. fold at one end. Fold the square accordion-style, working from one end toward the other.

3. After you fold up the entire square, fold the pleated strip in half crosswise. Staple the inner edges together.

4. Holding the inner corners, pull the pleats out to make a fan shape.

5. For pinwheels: Make two half-circle fans and staple them together on the edges. You might also want to staple smaller pinwheels in the center of larger ones.

6. To hang a pinwheel, punch a hole at the top. Loop string or ribbon through and knot.

Super Star Shells

Transform beach shells and starfish into a sparkly centerpiece or a shiny paperweight. You'll love how pretty the shells look after they're covered in glitter.

WHAT YOU NEED

bucket of soapy water
bleach
seashells and dried starfish
plate
Mod Podge glue
medium paintbrush
glitter in assorted colors
spoons

HOW TO MAKE

1. Clean seashells and starfish in a bucket of warm soapy water and a couple capfuls of bleach. Just let them soak, then rinse them off. You can also bleach shells to pure white by soaking them overnight in a mixture of equal parts bleach and water. Make sure there is enough water to cover the whole shell. Let dry for 24 hours.

2. Use the paintbrush to spread a thin layer of glue on the shells in the spots where you want to add glitter. Sprinkle a spoonful or two of glitter onto the glued area. Shake off excess glitter and let dry.

3. If you want to use more than one color, spread glue on another spot. Spoon on glitter in a different color. Shake off excess glitter and let dry. Repeat this step until you've made the design you want.

Glam Clam Paperweight

Glitter up a shell to make a shiny gift for a teacher, Grandma, or friend. This is a great project to do with a group too.

WHAT YOU NEED

	large scallop shell
1 to 2 c	plaster of paris
	bowl and spoon

HOW TO MAKE

1 Follow the instructions for Super Star Shells (see page 82) to decorate the outside of the scallop shell.

2 Following the directions on the package, mix up plaster of paris. To make the paperweight, turn shell over and spoon the plaster of paris into the shell to fill. Smooth the top; let dry.

Starring You Frame

Start with a plain frame or recycle an old one into this starfish-studded wonder. A bright palette of glitter provides the unexpected punch.

WHAT YOU NEED

	wooden frame
	Mod Podge glue
	foam paintbrush
	extra-fine glitter
	craft glue
	hot-glue gun
25	mini dried starfish or small shells

HOW TO MAKE

1 GROWN-UPS: First remove backing and glass from frame; you'll work with the wooden part only.

2 Using the foam paintbrush, cover the frame with a thin layer of glue. Sprinkle on glitter. Let dry.

3 Following the instructions for Super Star Shells (see page 82), decorate the starfish or shells.

4 GROWN-UPS: Help kids with this step. Using a hot-glue gun, glue starfish and shells to the frame. Let dry.

Royal (Icing) Sand Castle

Everyone will have the royal giggles while making the kingdom's walls out of graham crackers and the heavenly spires out of ice cream cones.

WHAT YOU NEED

1 box graham crackers
X-Acto knife
cake icing in 2 to 3 colors
freezer bags
1 box sugar ice cream cones
colorful paper
glue
toothpick
colored sugar
assorted candies

HOW TO MAKE

1 For each small building: Break 2 large graham crackers in half, making four 4x4 squares. For tower, use 4 large graham crackers. GROWN-UPS: With an X-Acto knife, carefully cut openings for windows. Also cut another cracker into 12 small squares for roof decoration for each building.

2 Make a pastry bag: Fill a freezer bag half-full with icing and cut a small hole in a corner of the bag.

3 Create a building by making a box out of the graham cracker squares, using the icing as "glue": On each of the 4 squares, pipe icing on 3 edges. Prop one square on its unpiped edge; "attach" the next square perpendicular to it, pressing lightly so icing will stick. Add other crackers on the sides to complete the box.

4 Break another cracker in half. Lay one of the halves on top of the box to create a roof. Pipe icing in the center of the roof and set an ice cream cone on top of the icing. Pipe icing around the cone and onto the roof's edges. Place 12 small squares in the icing, 3 per side.

5 For the flags, cut out a triangle shape from paper. Apply a thin layer of glue to half of it, and then fold it around a toothpick.

6 Put a blob of icing on top of the cone; place the flag in the icing.

7 Decorate the castle and its grounds with assorted candies and colored sugar. It's your royal kingdom, so you can use any kind of candy you want!

Ocean in a Jar

Imagine a lava lamp the color of the deep blue sea, and you'll have an inkling of how intrigued you'll be when you shake this jar up and watch the slow-moving waves inside.

WHAT YOU NEED

bucket of soapy water
bleach
clear glass jar with a tight-fitting lid
seashells and dried starfish
blue food coloring
½ c   vegetable oil
hot-glue gun

HOW TO MAKE

1. Clean seashells and starfish in a bucket of warm soapy water and a couple capfuls of bleach. Just let them soak, then rinse them off. You can also bleach shells to pure white by soaking them overnight in a mixture of equal parts bleach and water. Make sure there is enough water to cover the whole shell. Let dry for 24 hours.

2. Fill the jar with cold water. Add the shells, 2 to 3 drops of blue food coloring, and vegetable oil to the jar; adjust color and oil, adding more if needed.

3. GROWN-UPS: To seal the lid of the jar, heat one stick of glue in the hot-glue gun; apply the glue to the top edge of the jar, then quickly place lid on jar. Once cool, peel excess glue from outside the jar.

4. Shake and watch—the oil in the water moves slowly and mysteriously!

By the Sea Sand Art

Sand art is a craft beloved by all ages, and these simple bottles have a kind of mod appeal. Prep a couple of different sand colors so you'll have lots of options as you create your designs.

WHAT YOU NEED

- large paper cups
- fine sand
- water
- green, blue, and yellow food coloring
- plastic spoons
- paper towels
- glass bottle with cork or jar with lid
- bamboo skewers

HOW TO MAKE

For sand

1. Fill each paper cup halfway with sand.

2. Add enough water to each cup to completely cover the sand.

3. Add a few drops of food coloring to each cup to get the desired colors.

4. Stir each cup with a plastic spoon and set aside for a half hour while the sand absorbs the color.

5. Pour the excess water off the sand. Scoop the sand out onto paper towels and allow the sand to dry completely. GROWN-UPS: You may want to prep the colored sand the day before, to make sure it's completely dry before calling kids to the craft table.

For sand art

1. The effect will differ depending on the shape of your jar or bottle, but the technique is the same. Add layers of different colored sand to create a pattern. You can make straight horizontal layers, or change the pattern by tilting the bottle/jar as you pour another layer or poking a bamboo skewer along the edges after each layer to create a wavy effect.

2. Fill to the top and screw lid on jar or place cork in the top of the bottle.

FALL
fUN FOR EVERYone

HALLOWEEN

Step right up for a host of trick-or-treat projects, including papier-mâché jack-o'-lanterns, creepy cup lights, and spidery jack-o'-lanterns. Get into the fun by wrapping yourself up like a mummy (see page 110), and let the fright-night festivities begin!

Jack-o'-Lanterns

All Hallow's Eve brings more than just costumes and candy—there are lots of enjoyable crafts to do too. Pick out a big, fat pumpkin and draw a toothy grin or a black widow spider on it to cut out (hey, you could do them both!).

WHAT YOU NEED

pumpkin (we used Funkin artificial
    pumpkins from www.funkins.com)
spoon
black fine-tip marker
stencil paper
pencil
scissors
straight pins
sharp paring knife
serrated pumpkin-carving tool (optional)

HOW TO MAKE

1. If you're using a real pumpkin, cut a circle around the top of the stem, remove (and keep) top, then clean out the seeds and contents inside with a large spoon.

2. There are different ways to create a design on your pumpkin. You can draw a design freehand with a black fine-tip marker. Or you can copy the spider and spiderweb templates on page 203 onto stencil paper. Depending on the size of your pumpkin, you may want to enlarge the stencils on a photocopier. Or go online and download stencils (www.pumpkincarving101.com and www.pumpkinmasters.com are two good sites to check out).

3. Place stencil or template on the pumpkin and hold it in place using straight pins. With a sharp paring knife, carve around the stencil or your own design. Cut finer details using a serrated pumpkin-carving tool.

4. When you're finished, place the stemmed top of your pumpkin back in place.

It's Pumpkin Time

Surprise! These Halloween lanterns are made by covering a balloon with papier-mâché— and then popping it! The expressions on the faces can be as silly or as scary as you want— after all, it is the spookiest night of the year.

WHAT YOU NEED

- flour
- water
- plastic bucket
- balloons
- newspaper torn into 3 x 5-in. strips
- string
- clothesline
- straight pin
- X-Acto knife
- orange acrylic paint
- medium paintbrush
- black tissue paper
- Mod Podge glue
- Phillips head screwdriver
- orange pipe cleaner
- string of lights

HOW TO MAKE

1. Mix 2 c flour with 2 c water in plastic bucket to make a thick paste. You may need to make more of this mixture depending on how many jack-o'-lanterns you want to make.

2. Blow up a balloon and tie a knot on the top. Take strips of newspaper and dip into the papier-mâché paste; apply one at a time to the balloon, overlapping pieces and covering it completely with 3 to 4 layers. Cut a 2-in. length of string and tie to the knot on the balloon. Hang it on the clothesline to dry for a day or two. Repeat this step to make however many pumpkins you want.

3. When pumpkin is completely dry, pop the balloon with the straight pin. With the X-Acto knife, cut an opening at the top to poke a light through.

4. Paint outside of pumpkin with acrylic paint and let dry on clothesline for at least 1 hour.

5. From black tissue paper, cut out two triangles for eyes, a longer triangle for nose, and a jagged grin for the jack-o'-lantern's mouth. For a long-lasting pumpkin that has a nice glow, coat it with glue to seal the paint.

6. With the screwdriver, poke two holes about ¾-in. apart on either side of the opening on the pumpkin. Cut the pipe cleaner in half and guide the pieces up and out through the holes. Twist once. Hang on string of lights as shown, twisting the pipe cleaner around the light to hang.

NOTE: Never leave a string of lights on when unattended.

Creepy Cup Lights

Jack-o'-lantern faces look cool when you cut little eyes, noses, and smiles out for these simple-to-make orange or black decorations for Halloween.

WHAT YOU NEED
fine-tip black or silver markers
orange or black paper cups
X-Acto knife
string of lights

HOW TO MAKE
1. Draw jack-o'-lanterns on cups.

2. GROWN-UPS: Use an X-Acto knife to cut out the faces. Also cut an X on the bottom of each cup. This is where the lights will poke through.

3. When attaching the cups to the string of lights, make sure that the bulbs do not touch the sides of the cups.

NOTE: Never leave a string of lights on when unattended.

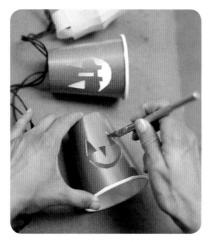

Ghoulish Glows

Use tulle, cellophane, or tissue paper to turn jelly jars or a glass votive into spooky lights.

WHAT YOU NEED
squares of cellophane, tulle, or tissue paper in Halloween colors
clean glass jelly jars with paper labels removed or round glass votive holders
ribbons
glue
plastic spiders
tea lights

HOW TO MAKE
1. Cut cellophane, tulle, or tissue paper to cover the outside of jar or glass votive.

2. Wrap the material around the jar (keeping it away from the mouth of the jar). Tie ribbon tightly around rim to hold material in place and knot.

3. Glue plastic spiders to the front of the jar or the ribbon trim.

4. Insert a tea light. Make sure no material hangs over opening before lighting the candle.

NOTE: Never leave candles lit when unattended.

Lickety-Split Ghosts

Make at least a dozen of these candy ghosts to hang up around the house. You may find they start mysteriously disappearing one by one before the Halloween season ends.

WHAT YOU NEED

For one ghost
- lollipop
- 10-in. square of white fabric
- 11-in. square of cheesecloth
- white ribbon or twine
- glue-on eyes
- tacky glue
- scissors
- fishing line

HOW TO MAKE

1. Layer the square of cheesecloth on the square of fabric and wrap them around the head of the lollipop. Gather at the neck and tie with white ribbon or twine.

2. Glue on eyes and let dry.

3. Cut a long piece of fishing line and loop it through the cheesecloth at the very top of the ghost; knot. Hang in your window, on the porch, or around the house.

Trick-or-Treat Eats

Concoct this creepy-looking snack for a Halloween party. Start the night before to let the tapioca soak in cold water overnight.

WHAT YOU NEED

For eight 6-oz. servings

	medium bowls
8 oz.	box small pearl tapioca
3 qt.	water
2½ c	sugar
3	cinnamon sticks
½ t	green food coloring
	lemon/lime soda or ginger ale
24	gummy worms

HOW TO MAKE

1. In a medium bowl, cover tapioca with cold water; refrigerate overnight.

2. In a 6-qt. pot, bring the water, sugar, cinnamon, and coloring to a boil. Stir until sugar dissolves. Drain tapioca, then add to the pot. Bring to a second boil. Reduce heat to medium-high and gently boil, stirring occasionally, 16 to 18 minutes, until tapioca is almost translucent.

3. Remove from heat; let stand 20 minutes, until completely translucent. Place a colander in a bowl and drain the tapioca, reserving 1 c of the liquid; discard cinnamon. Transfer tapioca to another bowl with reserved liquid; stir. (Recipe can be made ahead to this point; refrigerate, covered, for up to 2 days.)

4. Before serving, add a drop or two of soda to tapioca. Spoon into eight 6-oz. plastic tumblers. Arrange 3 worms in each. Add more soda to taste.

Inspire shrieks and "eeks" with jars full of gooey eyeballs (grapes with cloves in green gelatin) and slimy guts (cooked spaghetti). Add food coloring to make them look really icky! For more creepy ideas and recipes, turn to page 199.

Hostess-with-the-Ghostest Bowl

You would never guess this ghost is made from wire hangers and a couple of Styrofoam balls—or that it's really a cinch to do. Fill it with candy before the trick-or-treaters arrive.

WHAT YOU NEED

2 wire coat hangers
    large bowls
    white glue
    Styrofoam balls
    foam-core board
    pencil
    X-Acto knife
    masking tape
    scissors
1 yard of white cotton fabric
    water
    black felt

HOW TO MAKE

1. Bend one hanger to stand over the bowl. Bend the second hanger to make the ghost's arms as shown.

2. Tape the hangers together at the top, where the ghost's head will be, and at the sides, where the ghost's arms will be. Glue Styrofoam balls in place, at the ghost's head and arms.

3. With a pencil, trace a circle on foam-core board using a large bowl as a template. Cut out with X-Acto knife. Place bowl with wire hangers on top of the board.

4. Tape the wire stand into place on the board.

5. Cut a large circle from your fabric. The quickest and easiest way to do this is to fold the fabric in half from top to bottom. Cut a half circle.

6. Mix 1 c white glue and ½ c water in the large bowl. Soak the fabric circle in the mixture until fully saturated.

7. Drape the fabric over the ghost frame and allow the section between the arms to fall into the bowl. Fold the raw edge of the fabric under and glue to the board. Let dry.

8. When your project is completely dry, cut two ovals of black felt and glue on the head for eyes.

Spooky Paint

Have some fun before Halloween by decorating windows with a ghost, black cat, jack-o'-lantern, or haunted house. The best part is the easy cleanup for you—the soap is already in the paint!

WHAT YOU NEED

½ T   powdered tempera paint
1 T   clear dishwashing liquid
        artist paintbrushes

HOW TO MAKE

1. Mix the powdered paint with dishwashing liquid until it resembles house paint.

2. Paint a holiday scene on the inside of your windows. For a little extra help, tape a picture to the outside of the window and follow along inside with the paints.

3. When you're ready to remove, clean the paint off with water. For streak and lint-free windows, try cleaning glass with a page from an old newspaper.

Mummy Dearest

Back from the land of the dead, His Creepiness looks like he's brought a few icky spider friends along! This surprisingly simple costume is big fun for young and old, especially if everyone helps.

WHAT YOU NEED

scissors
white or cream thermal long johns
5 to 6 yds. off-white cotton or
polyester-blend jersey
safety pins
rubber spiders
white sneakers

HOW TO MAKE

1. Cut fabric into 4- to 6-in.-wide strips.

2. Have mummy put on long john bottoms. Start at the ankles: Wrap strips of fabric around the legs and secure with a safety pin. Keep wrapping the mummy's "bandages" over the hips and up to the waist.

3. Have mummy put on the top. Wrap the arms first, then start at the bottom of the top and work up. Secure with safety pins.

4. Tie pieces randomly. Add a few knots here and there—or wrap pieces on the diagonal. Leave a few strips loose.

5. Get creative and glue rubber spiders on the mummy's bandages in a random fashion. Wrap strips around hands and the head.

6. When your mummy is ready to return to the land of the living, undo safety pins and unwrap strips. Depending on how tightly you've wrapped the strips, you may be able to take off the bottoms without unpinning.

HALLOWEEN
Miss Lazy Daisy

There's no trick to making this cutie-patootie costume from fabric and foam—only a big treat for everyone who sees it! Start it a few days before Halloween night so it's in full bloom right on time.

WHAT YOU NEED

	fabric pencil
2 yds.	yellow stretch fabric
	scissors
	sewing machine
	thread (yellow, dark green, light green, and brown)
1 yd.	dark-green stretch fabric
1 yd.	lime-green stretch fabric
2 yds.	brown stretch fabric
3 yds.	1 in. foam padding
	polyester batting
2 yds.	1 in.-wide green elastic
	green sweatshirt
	beige tights

HOW TO MAKE

1. Go to page 202 for all the templates for this project. Follow instructions for enlarging templates so that face template will measure about 20 in. across and wrist template will measure about 10 in. across. For face: Lay two layers of yellow fabric over foam padding and pin in place. Trace the outline of the flower onto fabric. Machine stitch through all three layers following the outline of the flower. Cut out flower along the stitching line, leaving ¼-in. seam.

2. In the center, cut a 5-in. hole or an opening that is the right size to fit your child's face. Now you turn the top layer of yellow fabric right side out to enclose the foam. Pin in place and hand-stitch edges of center closed. Finally, machine stitch ¼ in. around edge of flower, then stitch lines of petal.

3. Repeat using smaller template to make two wrist flowers, cutting a 1¼-in. hole in the center, or size to fit your child's wrist.

4. Enlarge leaf templates so that leaves are about 30 in. long. Repeat same procedure as for flowers, placing one layer of dark-green fabric and one of lime-green fabric over foam, tracing, then stitching outline of leaf through all three layers. Leave a small section along one edge of leaf open for turning. After turning the leaf right side out, hand-stitch opening closed. Machine-stitch vein down center of each leaf. Make two leaves.

5. Enlarge templates for the flowerpot and rim in proportion to the size of your child. Place two layers of brown fabric over foam; pin and cut out flowerpot and rim. Stitch along top, bottom, and one side of each piece; turn so foam is encased in fabric; stitch raw edge closed. Sew the rim to the top of the pot.

6. Sew the two leaves to the inside of the pot.

7. Cut two 22-in. lengths of elastic to make straps, or size to fit your child. Sew one end of each strap inside the front of the pot. Attach straps in back using large safety pins to adjust height of pot on your child. Cut two 10-in. pieces of elastic to hold flower headpiece in place. Attach the first piece from ear to ear in back. Attach the second piece from center of forehead to the crosspiece of elastic.

Creepy, Crawly Spider

Construct this adorable arachnid with batting, fake fur, and a few pairs of gloves—and make all those polyester superheroes marvel at your ingenuity.

3	black sweatshirts
	scissors
3	pairs white gloves
	polyester batting
1 yd.	faux fur
	large-eye sewing or upholstery needle
1½ yds.	fishing line
	black baseball cap
2	small round nylon sponges
	black paint
	hot-glue gun

HOW TO MAKE

1. First, you'll make two pairs of the spider's crawly arms: Cut sleeves from 2 sweatshirts and stuff 2 pairs of white gloves with batting. Stitch gloves to the wrists of the loose sleeves. Firmly stuff arms with batting so they stick straight out, then attach the spider's arms to each side of the remaining sweatshirt, one set at the waist and the other right below the armholes.

2. Next, you'll add a little fuzzy fur to the spider's arms and neck. Cut 2½-in. strips of faux fur. Stitch them to the collar and at the shoulder, elbow, and wrist of each of the six arms.

3. Thread needle with fishing line, and attach wrists of each set of arms to the arms below with 6-in. lengths of line.

4. For the spider's head, cut the visor off the baseball cap. Cut small pieces of faux fur and glue onto cap to cover it completely. For eyes, dip sponges in black acrylic paint; let dry, and glue to the front of the cap.

Put on Your Poker Face

It's your lucky day: Take a deck of cards and choose a favorite to turn into one of these clever costumes. Whichever you choose will show off your winning hand—at crafts, that is!

WHAT YOU NEED

deck of cards
X-Acto knife
piece of foam core cut to fit your child
glue or spray adhesive
heavy-duty self-adhesive Velcro
sweatshirt
needle and thread or safety pins (optional)
red or black felt
cardboard
red or black hat

HOW TO MAKE

1. Once you know what card you want to make, have your local copy shop enlarge the playing card to fit on the piece of foam core.

2. Working in a well-ventilated area, spread a thin layer of glue or spray adhesive on the foam core. Carefully place the photocopy of the card on it, smoothing out any wrinkles in the paper.

3. To attach the card to the sweatshirt, stick an 8-in. strip of Velcro on the back of the card and another on the sweatshirt. To make sure the card stays put, tack Velcro securely to the sweatshirt with a needle and thread or safety pins. Put sweatshirt on before you stick the playing card to it.

4. Top off your card costume with a cute matching hat that ties in with the suit and color of the card you've chosen. Cut two symbols in the shape of a diamond, club, spade, or heart—one in red or black felt and one in cardboard. Use glue or spray adhesive to attach felt symbol to cardboard, then stick a 2-in. strip of Velcro on the back of the cardboard and another on the hat. Stick symbol to the hat.

EXPIRES   11 01 08

HALLOWEEN
Milk & Cookies

Halloween brings a lot of sweets, but this yummy cookie-and-milk duo is the sweetest of them all. Everyone can get in on the act by helping glue the sugary sprinkles or colorful lettering onto the costumes.

WHAT YOU NEED

For milk container

> X-Acto knife
> white 3-piece folding foam display board
> red construction paper
> scissors
> precut block lettering
> tacky glue
> white face paint (optional)

For cookie costume

> scissors
2 yds. pink fleece
1 yd. light-tan fleece
> 48 x 1 x 24-in. piece of foam
> pins
> sewing machine or needle and thread
> spray adhesive
> tacky glue
> felt "sprinkles"
3 yds. pink ribbon

HOW TO MAKE

For milk container

1. Cut out openings for arms with the X-Acto knife on opposite sides of the display board. Have your child try it on by putting his or her arms in the holes. Mark two places: Where the board hits at the knees, so you can cut the bottom of the board horizontally, and where your child's face is, so you can cut a round opening for the face.

2. At the top, cut the sides on an angle so they look like a milk carton.

3. Using scissors, cut stripes and blocks out of the red construction paper to create the milk-carton design. Glue the red shapes and block lettering onto the foam board.

4. You can use white face paint so your child has a "milky" complexion. And while white gloves and red pants are optional, they make the costume look fantastic!

For cookie costume

1. For the cream filling, cut two 24-in. pink fleece circles.

2. For the cookies, cut two 24-in. light-tan fleece circles.

3. Cut two 22-in. foam circles for padding.

4. For the icing, cut one 16-in. pink fleece circle with a wavy edge.

5. Place one 24-in. pink circle and one 24-in. light-tan circle right sides together and stitch, leaving a 10-in opening. Turn the circles right side out, insert one piece of foam, and hand-stitch the opening closed.

6. Using spray adhesive, affix the pink icing to the light-tan fleece. Use tacky glue to affix sprinkles to the icing.

7. For the ties that hold the cookie on the shoulders, cut two 27-in.-long pieces of ribbon, and hand-stitch the ends of each to the strawberry cream side of the cookie, close to the edge and about 7 in. apart.

8. To make the back of the cookie, repeat Steps 5 and 7 (but not Step 6). Tie the front and back of the cookie together and over the child's shoulders.

Stop & Go

Full speed ahead: These eye-catching costumes take an afternoon to assemble— and there's plenty to keep hands busy, from choosing which road sign to make to tying the elastic on the cone-hat.

WHAT YOU NEED

picture of a road sign
X-Acto knife
piece of foam core cut to fit your child
glue or spray adhesive
heavy-duty self-adhesive Velcro
sweatshirt
needle and thread or safety pins (optional)
awl
small traffic cone (available at a toy store)
elastic or string

HOW TO MAKE

1. Download a copy of the road sign you want to make (try www.images.google.com and type in "road signs"). Have your local copy shop enlarge the image to fit on the piece of foam core.

2. Working in a well-ventilated area, spread a thin layer of glue or spray adhesive on the foam core. Carefully place the photocopy of the road sign on it, smoothing out any wrinkles in the paper.

3. To attach the foam core to the sweatshirt, stick a 6-in. strip of Velcro on the back of the sign and another on the child's sweatshirt. For extra reinforcement, tack Velcro to the sweatshirt with a needle and thread or safety pins. Stick the road sign to the sweatshirt.

4. To make the hat, poke holes on two sides of the traffic cone with an awl. Thread elastic or string through the holes, and tie the string under the child's chin.

Paper Bag Turkey

Fancy-schmancy centerpieces are nice sometimes, but this Mr. Turkey, made out of a couple of paper bags, draws the whole family into the spirit of the Thanksgiving holiday.

WHAT YOU NEED

2 flat brown paper bags, 1 large and 1 smaller (NOT flat-bottomed grocery bags)
  newspaper
  masking tape
  scissors
10 brown pipe cleaners
  craft glue
  construction paper in orange, brown, red, and yellow
2 tiny brown or black pom-poms

HOW TO MAKE

1. Open the large bag. Stuff the bag with newspaper and shape the bag to look like a turkey body with the tail pointing up—make sure you also shape it so that it will sit on a table. Leave enough of the bag empty so that you can twist the opening into a neck. Once twisted, secure the twist with masking tape.

2. Do the same thing with the smaller bag (for the head), but form the head to create a beak from one of the corners of the bag. Tuck the other corner on the top of the head to hide it.

3. Take the two bags by their necks and join them together with masking tape. You may have to trim the bags a bit for the proper proportion of the head to the body. Cover the neck with the pipe cleaners by wrapping them around the neck, then twisting one into the next. Trim off any excess on the pipe cleaners. Secure the last one with glue.

4. Cut turkey feathers out of the construction paper and attach to the back of the turkey with glue. Cut a waddle out of the red paper and attach it under the chin with glue. With the brown paper, make a small cone and attach it to the head for a beak. Glue the tiny pom-poms onto the turkey's face for eyes.

Leaf Menagerie

It's hard to resist bringing back leaves from a hike, so why not put them to good use? Spend an afternoon using Mother Nature's bright fall foliage to make a collage or two suitable for framing.

WHAT YOU NEED

- brown kraft paper cut to 8½ x 11 in. or sized to fit your frame
- masking tape
- a variety of autumn leaves
- twigs
- craft glue
- brown crayon
- paintbrush
- brown paint
- wooden frame

HOW TO MAKE

1. Place the brown paper on the table and tape the corners down.

2. Using the leaves and twigs, make an animal, bird, butterfly, or face (or whatever inspires you when you look at the leaf shapes).

3. Glue the leaves into position; let dry. Add any details with a brown crayon, if desired.

4. GROWN-UPS: Remove glass and backing from frame; paint the frame. Let dry. Do not replace glass; place collage on backing and place inside of frame.

Falling Leaves Banner

This easy-to-sew banner is a neat way to signal the turn of the seasons and would be a welcome gift for a Thanksgiving host.

WHAT YOU NEED

felt in a variety of autumnal colors
scissors
craft glue
thick yarn or string
4 buttons
12-in. dowel with ½-in. diameter

HOW TO MAKE

1. For the base of the banner: Cut a piece of felt into an 11 x 17-in. rectangle.

2. Trace real leaves or use the leaf templates on page 203; cut leaves out of the other colors of felt. Places leaves on the banner base and decide on your design. Glue in place.

3. Cut pieces of yarn to run along the edges of the banner; cross at the corners where they meet. Glue in place. Glue buttons on the corners.

4. Cut two 2 x 4-in. pieces of felt for the hangers. Fold in half and glue to the backside of the banner. Let dry completely before hanging.

5. Slip the dowel through the hangers.

Lots To do in WINTER

HOLIDAYS
- Ho-Ho-Ho Garlands
- Let's Have a Ball! Ornaments
- Kid-Friendly Garlands
- Very Merry Magnet Frames
- Holiday Hang-Ups
- Soapsuds Snowmen
- Cinnamon Clay Classics
- Glitter Globes
- Kwanzaa Mkeka Mat
- Shining Stars
- Spice of Life Cutouts

NEW YEAR'S EVE
- New Year's Noisemakers

VALENTINE'S DAY
- My Funny Valentine & Forever Yours Wreath
- Make-My-Day Bouquet
- Heart-to-Heart Garland
- Tokens of Affection

Ho-Ho-Ho Garlands

Get into the spirit of the season: Gather a few supplies and grab our easy instructions for making these cute snowman and snowflake crafts to decorate your tree.

WHAT YOU NEED
For let-it-snow garlands
newspaper
wooden snowflakes
  (available in craft stores)
Mod Podge glue
small paintbrush
white glitter
white string

For pom-pom snowmen
large needle
white pom-poms in different sizes
kite string
black and orange Fimo clay
toothpick
craft glue

HOW TO MAKE
For let-it-snow garlands
1. Cover the work area with newspaper for easy cleanup.

2. Spread a thin layer of glue on snowflakes and sprinkle a little bit of glitter on them. Shake off extra glitter and let dry.

3. Glue snowflakes onto string, spacing them equal distances apart.

For pom-pom snowmen
1. Create a garland of small pom-poms by threading them onto string with a needle.

2. For snowmen: Thread small, medium, and large pom-poms together from bottom to top, leaving enough string to add hat and tie figure onto the garland.

3. Make a snowman hat by flattening a small ball of clay into a circle to create a base. Roll another piece of clay between hands into a long tube. Slice off a piece and stick the hat on the base.

4. Poke a hole with a toothpick in the center of the hat base and through the top of it, so that after it's baked, you can thread string through it to hang.

5. Make eyes, carrot nose, and buttons out of clay. Bake pieces of clay according to package instructions. Let cool before applying.

6. Use a dab of glue to affix eyes and carrot nose to snowman's face, and attach buttons to middle pom-pom. Thread hats onto snowmen.

7. Space snowmen equal distances apart on the pom-pom garland and attach, using the remaining thread.

Let's Have a Ball! Ornaments

Sure, papier-mâché can get a little messy, but this is a neater way to do it—and a fun project for kids that allows them to put their own personal stamp on these festive holiday balls.

WHAT YOU NEED
For 1 ball
- string
- pipe cleaner
- 4-in. Styrofoam ball
- newspaper
- medium paintbrush
- Mod Podge glue
- red and green acrylic paint
- dot stickers (available at office-supply stores)
- decorative-edge scissors
- white, green, and red construction paper
- colorful thin ribbon

HOW TO MAKE

1. Create a short "clothesline" with string for hanging your wet ornament. (It's surprising how kids love to do stuff like this!)

2. Then form a hanger for the ornament: Cut a 4-in. piece of pipe cleaner, bend it in half, and insert ends close together into the Styrofoam ball.

3. For papier-mâché: Tear small (3-in.) pieces of newspaper.

4. Spread a thin layer of glue, using the paintbrush, on half of the ball; papier-mâché that half with pieces of newspaper. Repeat on the other side.

5. Thread the ball onto the "clothesline" and let dry until it no longer feels sticky.

6. Bring the ball back to the worktable and apply a coat of paint; return it to the string and let dry. Repeat until you're satisfied with the color.

7. Now it's time to dress up the ball with dots, circles, or cut-up pieces of construction paper with dabs of glue.

8. To protect the ball and give it a glossy sheen, coat it with a layer of glue. Hang it on the string; let dry, then coat it with glue one more time. Let dry completely. Tie ribbon on hanger.

Kid-Friendly Garlands

'Tis the season to be jolly—and everyone will be happy creating these bright garlands with colorful beads and fancy paper.

WHAT YOU NEED

For folded-paper chains

assorted sheets of patterned paper

scissors

For pipe cleaner chains

colorful pipe cleaners

scissors

colorful plastic beads

craft glue

HOW TO MAKE

For folded-paper chains

1 Cut sheets of patterned paper into 7 x 1¼-in. strips.

2 Show kids how to do this simple fold according to the diagram at right: Fold each strip lengthwise, forming a thin strip. Fold that strip once crosswise, forming a 3½ x ⅝-in. rectangle. Unfold crosswise, leaving folded lengthwise. Fold ends in so they meet at center crease, then fold them once again to form a rectangle. Start by making about 15 to 20 rectangles.

3 How to make the Folded-Paper Chain: Hold 1 rectangle sideways, then slide the sides of another rectangle into the folds of the first rectangle. Repeat until the chain is the length you want.

For pipe cleaner chains

1 Plan a color scheme for your chain— you can use lots of different colors or choose 2 different colors of pipe cleaners, like we did. Cut pipe cleaners in half.

2 Take two pipe cleaners and twist together lengthwise. Make a few dozen of these twists or make however many you want, depending on the length of your garland.

3 Slide colorful beads into the middle of each twist and then bend the twist into a circle.

4 Put a drop of glue on both tips of one twist, and then tuck the tips into the beads of a second twist. Repeat this step, adding more twists onto the first one, until your chain is the length you want.

Very Merry Magnet Frames

After making a few frames, slip in your favorite photos and turn the fridge into a holiday gallery.

WHAT YOU NEED

square or rectangle frame for tracing
paper
pencil
scissors
craft foam in green and red
decorative-edge scissors
X-Acto knife
ruler
craft glue
hole punch
1½ yds. ⅛-in. ribbon
clear acetate sheet
self-adhesive magnetic sheet

HOW TO MAKE

1 To make a template, find a frame that's the size you want and trace its outline onto a piece of paper. Cut out the template and you're ready to begin.

2 Place template on foam and cut out the frame, using decorative-edge scissors. To cut out the inside edge of the frame, use the X-Acto knife and ruler (rather than scissors) for a neat, even finish. Be sure to save this piece!

3 You can also make a slightly fancier frame by cutting 4 narrow foam strips with the decorative-edge scissors. Glue these pieces on the inner edges of the frame and let dry.

4 Use the hole punch to make a row of holes along the sides of the frame or just at the corners (see picture, right). Loop ribbon through holes and tie, either on the front or back of the frame—it's your call.

5 Cut a piece of acetate to fit over the opening of the frame. Glue in place on front of the frame and let dry at least 2 hours.

6 Apply the sticky side of a magnetic sheet to 1 side of the reserved foam piece, and trim the magnetic sheet so it's the same size as the foam.

7 Use this magnetic-backed foam piece to make the slot on back where you slide in your photo: Glue 3 edges on the foam side (not the magnetic!) and stick onto the back of the frame. Let dry 24 hours.

8 You may need to trim your photo a bit to slip it into the slot on the back.

Holiday Hang-Ups

You'll find these adorable snowmen just as much fun to make as the real ones. Use them as gift tags or as a cute way to hang holiday cards around the house.

WHAT YOU NEED

For 2 snowmen

- juice glass
- small votive
- pencil
- craft foam in white, black, and orange
- scissors
- hole punch
- craft glue
- black pipe cleaners
- permanent pen
- plaid or checkered ribbon
- wooden or wire clothespins

HOW TO MAKE

1 Use a juice glass and small votive to trace a snowman shape onto the white foam; cut out. Use scissors and cut black foam into the shape of a hat; cut a small triangle for the nose from the orange foam. Use the hole punch and black foam to make the eyes and buttons. Put a dab of glue on the back of hat, eyes, buttons, and nose and affix to the snowman.

2 Fashion pipe cleaner arms, cutting tiny pieces for fingers and twisting them onto the end of each arm. Glue arms on.

3 Complete the look by drawing a dotted smile onto the snowman's face with the pen. Tie a plaid or checkered ribbon into a bow at the neck.

4 If you're using these as gift tags, write *to* and *from* at the bottom of the snowman. If you're making your snowman into a decorative clip, glue a clothespin to the back, and let dry for 2 hours before using.

Soapsuds Snowmen

Bring winter inside with this "aw, that's cute!" centerpiece. This is a classic—and you already have the ingredients!

WHAT YOU NEED

	newspaper
4 c	white powdered laundry soap
	large mixing bowl
	electric mixer
1 c	cold water
	wooden skewer
	scissors
	clear glitter (optional)
	black construction paper
	craft glue
5	tiny black pom-poms
	orange craft foam or construction paper
	brown pipe cleaners
8 in.	½-in.-wide ribbon or felt

HOW TO MAKE

1 Cover the work area with newspaper for an easy cleanup.

2 Pour laundry soap into a large mixing bowl.

3 With the electric mixer on the lowest speed, slowly mix in cold water. Make sure to add the water only a tiny bit at a time.

4 When the mixture is the consistency of thick mud, it is time to get your hands wet. Roll handfuls of mixture into small, medium, and large balls. Stack your three "snowballs" into a snowman.

5 Using the skewer, poke holes on either side of the snowman's middle to make armholes. Then push the skewer down through the top of the head, joining the three sections of the snowman. Trim any excess skewer from the top.

6 If you want to make your snowman sparkle, sprinkle on some clear glitter.

7 Make a small top hat out of black construction paper by cutting a quarter-size circle and a nickel-size circle. Then cut a 2 x 3-in. piece and roll it into a tube; glue the edges together. Glue the smaller circle on top and the larger on the bottom for a brim. When the hat dries, glue it onto the snowman's head.

8 Once the snowman body is dry, glue on the tiny pom-poms for eyes and buttons. Cut a tiny triangle for a nose out of the orange foam or paper; glue it onto the face. Cut the pipe cleaners to use as arms and place into the holes.

9 Tie a piece of ribbon around the neck as a scarf.

Cinnamon Clay Classics

The house will feel all warm and cozy—and smell yummy, like cinnamon—when you make a batch of these clay people. Use these happy little ornaments to decorate your house during the holidays for years to come.

WHAT YOU NEED

To make 12 ornaments

1 c	ground cinnamon
¾ c	applesauce
	mixing bowl
	rolling pin
	bread board
	cookie cutters
	toothpick
	wire rack
	white squeeze paint
	thin cording, ribbon, or string

HOW TO MAKE

1. Mix the cinnamon and applesauce in a bowl. The mixture should have the consistency of dough.

2. Roll the dough out to a ¼-in. thickness on a board dusted with cinnamon.

3. Cut shapes from dough with cookie cutters.

4. Poke a hole at the top of the shape with a toothpick.

5. Allow the shapes to dry on a rack for several days, turning over every day.

6. When fully dry, decorate the ornaments with the squeeze paint. Let dry.

7. Pull string or ribbon through the hole and tie.

NOTE: Although these ornaments are made out of food, they are not edible.

Glitter Globes

Snow globes are magical—so create a little magic by making one. These are really special because you can pick out the sweet little treasures to place inside.

WHAT YOU NEED

> clean jars (with lids) large enough
>   to fit what you put inside
> assorted rubber toys
> hot-glue gun
> water
> glitter
> scissors
> felt

HOW TO MAKE

1. Glue the goodies to the inside of the lid.

2. Fill the jar with cold water (leave room for the water level to rise when the goodie is added). Add about a tablespoon of glitter.

3. Using the hot-glue gun, line the inside of the lid with glue and screw on lid. Apply a layer of glue around the rim of the lid to seal it in place.

4. Let it dry overnight—lid side up.

5. Cut a circle of felt to fit the top of the jar. Glue in place.

6. Shake—and watch it sparkle.

Kwanzaa Mkeka Mats

This is a great way to celebrate Kwanzaa, when friends and family join together to honor their African-American heritage. The colors of the mkeka (pronounced em-kay-kah) mat are symbolic—black, for the color of the people; red, for their struggle; green, for the future.

WHAT YOU NEED

For one place mat

- 12 x 16-in. piece each of red, green, and black felt
- ruler
- white pencil
- pinking shears (for fabric, not paper)
- black pen
- tacky craft glue

HOW TO MAKE

1. For each of the felt colors, using a ruler and white pencil, measure out 5 strips, each 2 x 16-in. long. Cut out each strip with the pinking shears.

2. Place the strips on a table, starting with green, then black, then red. Repeat this pattern until you have 7 strips across.

3. Using the remaining strips, weave strips horizontally (over and under the first set of strips), top to bottom, starting with green, then black, then red.

4. Trim the excess on the ends to create a place mat that measures approximately 13½ x 16 in.

5. To secure the strips, on each outside row, glue ends of each strip to the last cross-strip; let dry.

Shining Stars

Created out of wooden sticks, these easy-to-make Hanukkah stars are a fun project for everyone at a holiday get-together.

WHAT YOU NEED

wooden sticks in a variety of styles
    (wide tongue depressor, Popsicle sticks,
    coffee stirrers)
tacky craft glue
gold and silver spray paint or craft paint
paintbrushes
paper plates
glitter in gold and silver
thin gold and silver ribbon or string

HOW TO MAKE

1. Glue the sticks into triangles. Let dry.

2. Glue two triangles on top of each other, creating a Star of David. Let dry.
   Use glue to add details such as squiggly lines or circles. Let dry.

3. Paint the stars with the craft paint or spray paint. Let dry.

4. Place a star on a paper plate. Paint the star with a coat of glue and gently shake glitter over it until the star is covered. Tap the star lightly to remove excess glitter; place elsewhere to dry.

5. Glue and glitter all the stars, using the excess glitter from the star before.

6. Once dry, tie on a thin piece of ribbon for hanging.

Spice of Life Cutouts

Kids love to play with clay, and these simple Hanukkah cutouts made from cinnamon clay can be used as ornaments or gift tags.

WHAT YOU NEED

To make 12 ornaments

1 c	ground cinnamon
¾ c	applesauce
	mixing bowl
	rolling pin
	bread board
	Hanukkah cookie cutters
	toothpick
	wire rack
	blue squeeze paint
	thin cording, ribbon, or string

HOW TO MAKE

1. Mix the cinnamon and applesauce in a bowl. The mixture should have the consistency of dough.

2. Roll the dough out to a ¼-in. thickness on a board dusted with cinnamon.

3. Cut shapes from dough with cookie cutters.

4. Poke a hole at the top of the shape with a toothpick.

5. Allow the shapes to dry on a rack for several days, turning over every day.

6. When fully dry, decorate the ornaments with the squeeze paint. Let dry.

7. Pull string or ribbon through the hole and tie.

NOTE: Although these ornaments are made out of food, they are not edible.

New Year's Noisemakers

Noisy? Yup. And a whole lot of fun as well—
from making these crazy rattles to using them
to welcome in a brand-new year.

WHAT YOU NEED

plastic drinking cups (2 colors)
  or plastic bowls (2 colors)
hole punch
scissors
colored construction paper
quick-drying tacky craft glue
dried beans
pipe cleaners
dot stickers (available at office-supply stores)

HOW TO MAKE

1 Punch 3 evenly spaced holes ½ in. below
the rim of a plastic cup. Do the same for a
second cup, making sure that the holes
correspond to each other. (Punch 4 holes
if you are making the noisemaker from
the plastic bowls.)

2 Cut thin strips of colored paper and glue the
short ends along the lip of one cup or one
bowl. (When placing strips, make sure not to
cover up the holes.) Let dry.

3 Fill the cup or bowl with some beans; put
the second cup or bowl on top.

4 GROWN-UPS: Cut a pipe cleaner into thirds
with each piece about 4 in. long. Bend each
pipe cleaner into a C shape.

5 Take one pipe cleaner piece and thread it
through the hole on one cup, then through
the corresponding hole on the second cup;
pull together, and twist the pipe cleaner
closed on the outside of the cups. Repeat
for each hole.

6 Decorate with dot stickers.

My Funny Valentine

This little wreath is a project that's as simple as can be—it's easy for kids to make it with some loving guidance from a grown-up.

WHAT YOU NEED

hot-glue gun or craft glue
6- to 8-in. heart-shaped candy box
3 to 4 bags of red pistachios
1 yd. ribbon

HOW TO MAKE

1 You can make this project using almost any heart-shaped item as a base. Try a heart-shaped candy box or container.

2 Kids can use craft glue to cover the heart with pistachios, starting at the center. If you're using a hot-glue gun, grown-ups will have to supervise this step. Fold ribbon in half and glue to the top of the box. Be sure the glue is dry before hanging box up.

Forever Yours Wreath

Use any combination of flowers you like to make this beautiful wreath, but keep the colors of the blooms to pink and red for Valentine's Day.

WHAT YOU NEED

11 to 12 dozen pink and red flowers, real or fake
straight pins
12-in. heart-shaped moss wreath frame

HOW TO MAKE

1 If you're using real flowers, clip the stems off close to the base. We used ranunculus, but if they're not available, this wreath looks pretty in roses or fake flowers.

2 Attach each bud using a straight pin. Cover the front of the frame completely.

3 To keep the wreath fresh for 3 to 4 days, mist the flowers with cold water when you see them drooping. If it's warm or humid where you live, spritz once in the morning and once at night. If you're using fake flowers, there's no maintenance (maybe a quick dust-off), and it lasts forever!

Make-My-Day Bouquet

Real flowers fade, but these cuties stay alive for a long, long time—just like true love! (OK, that's corny.) Everyone will have fun making a bunch for a favorite teacher or friend.

WHAT YOU NEED

For one flower

- scissors
- assorted colored vellum and/or waxed papers
- heavy white paper
- wire
- button
- wire cutter
- craft glue
- green ribbon

HOW TO MAKE

1 Cut out hearts in 3 different sizes (4 or 5 hearts in each size) from vellum or waxed paper. Then cut out a small circle from the white paper.

2 To form the flowers, stack the "petals," starting with the large hearts, then medium-size ones, then small ones on top. Poke the wire through the circle and then through the stack of hearts at its tip.

3 Thread the wire through the button and twist to attach, then gently push petals forward so the button lies flush against them.

4 Snip wire to desired stem length with the wire cutters. Affix green ribbon to wire under white circle with glue. Wrap ribbon around the length of the wire and glue at the bottom of stem.

5 Arrange the petals so they look like a flower.

VALENTINE'S DAY

Heart-to-Heart Garland

These endearing hearts can be used in many ways—as a Valentine's card, perhaps? Create them out of red or pink paper or fabric, and string on a garland to brighten a room.

WHAT YOU NEED

    fusible interfacing
    fabrics
    iron
    standard or decorative-edge scissors
    hole punch
    string or twine

HOW TO MAKE

1. GROWN-UPS: With an iron, fuse the interfacing to the fabric.

2. Cut hearts in all different sizes from a variety of printed and solid fabrics.

3. Fuse small hearts onto larger ones or stack several onto each other and fuse. Make 14 hearts in different sizes, or however many you'd like for your garland.

4. Use the hole punch to make 2 holes on opposite sides near the top of each heart, then thread the string or twine through the holes.

VALENTINE'S DAY

Tokens of Affection

Here's a way to show love to family members or a favorite friend. Attach these pretty tags to a gift or use as decoration on a Valentine's Day card.

WHAT YOU NEED

- unwrapped crayons
- pencil sharpener or grater
- waxed paper
- craft or parchment paper
- iron
- scissors
- pen or marker
- X-Acto knife
- hole punch
- string or ribbon

HOW TO MAKE

1. Shred crayons one at a time using a grater or pencil sharpener onto a piece of waxed paper. Spread the shavings on the waxed paper, mixing colors if you want, and place another sheet of waxed paper on top. Then place a piece of craft or parchment over that. GROWN-UPS: Set your iron on low heat and carefully iron the waxed paper "sandwich," melting the crayon shavings. Set aside to cool and harden. Repeat with as many crayons as you like.

2. Discard the craft or parchment paper. Using scissors, cut the waxed-paper-and-crayon "sandwiches" into heart or gift-tag shapes. Sketch letters on shapes. GROWN-UPS: Cut letters out with an X-Acto knife.

3. Punch a hole in each tag. Loop string or ribbon through the hole and knot.

4. GROWN-UPS: Remember to clean your iron when you are finished with this project. HOW TO DO IT: Turn your iron up to high and iron over a piece of clean brown or white paper. Any wax deposits will melt off the iron onto the paper.

RaiNy Day
Play DATE

Baubles & Beads Mosaic Pots

What's cool about doing mosaics is you can glue almost anything—pieces of china, shells, stones, or bottle caps—onto the pot and it looks neat. Pick a color scheme to bring it all together—or just go crazy!

WHAT YOU NEED

terra-cotta flowerpots
small paintbrush
colorful acrylic craft paints
craft glue or hot-glue gun
small mosaic tiles
glass stones
beads

HOW TO MAKE

1 Paint the pots with the acrylic paint; let dry.

2 Glue the tiles, stones, and beads in a pattern or random design onto your pot. Let dry.

Flour Power Super Clay

Make this your "turn-to" activity when you can't think of anything else to do or if you want to make a gift for a friend before a visit. Chances are you have everything you need in your pantry and craft drawer.

WHAT YOU NEED

mixing bowl
1 c all-purpose flour
½ c salt
½ c very warm tap water
spoon
wire rack
acrylic craft paints
small paintbrush

HOW TO MAKE

1. Mix flour and salt.

2. Pour water into the mixture and stir.

3. Knead the mixture for a few minutes until smooth.

4. To make a candlestick holder, form a medium-size ball of clay. Flatten the ball into a circle, keeping the top slightly rounded. Make a circle in the center using a candle, or simply shape it with your fingers. For a little bowl, start with a medium-size ball of clay and flatten it into a circle. Roll another piece of clay between your hands until you have a long tube. Lay it on the circle, shaping and smoothing it onto the bottom until the side of the dish is formed.

5. Place on a wire rack and let air dry for a few days. You can also bake small pieces at 200 degrees for 2 hours. Let cool.

6. When dry or baked, paint the clay pieces and then let dry.

Sun Catcher Mobile

The more colorful you make this mobile, the better it will be to watch as it swings in the breeze. Use everyday objects—a juice glass, a dessert plate, or a top of a jar—to trace circles (how easy is that?).

WHAT YOU NEED

- unwrapped crayons
- pencil sharpener or grater
- waxed paper
- craft or parchment paper
- iron
- small plates, glasses, and bowls
- pencil
- scissors
- X-Acto knife
- small hole punch
- embroidery floss
- embroidery ring (available at craft stores)
- twine or thick cotton string

HOW TO MAKE

1. Using a pencil sharpener or grater, shred crayons one at a time onto a piece of waxed paper. Spread the shavings on the waxed paper, mixing colors if you want, and place another sheet of waxed paper on top. Then place a piece of craft or parchment over that. GROWN-UPS: Set your iron on low heat and carefully iron the waxed paper "sandwich," melting the crayon shavings. Set aside to cool and harden. Repeat with as many crayons as you like.

2. Once you have a few waxed paper colors, trace around household objects such as small plates, glasses, and bowls to create circles on the paper. Cut the large circles out with scissors. GROWN-UPS: Cut the centers out with an X-Acto knife.

3. Using the small hole punch, make a hole on the circle and string the embroidery floss through it. Cut the strings to various lengths.

4. Tie strings to the embroidery ring, varying the lengths, and knot in place.

5. Cut three pieces of the twine or cotton string. Tie each piece of twine on the embroidery ring a few inches apart. Gather twine at the top and knot all the ends together to hang.

6. GROWN-UPS: Remember to clean your iron when you are finished with this project. HOW TO DO IT: Turn your iron up to high and iron over a piece of clean brown or white paper. Any wax deposits will melt off the iron onto the paper.

Rope-It-In Basket

Sure, it looks like a work of art, but don't let it fool you: This is a great project for everyone. Yarn is the easiest material for young children to handle, but more experienced crafters might want to use ribbons or rope to create their own thing of beauty.

WHAT YOU NEED

balloon
small bowls
newspaper
yarn, rope, or ribbon
scissors
white glue
straight pin

HOW TO MAKE

1. Inflate balloon and place it in a bowl to keep it from rolling around while you work.

2. This project is messy to do, so put newspaper down before starting. Cut strips of yarn, rope, or ribbon and soak in a bowl of white glue.

3. Remove a piece of yarn from the bowl, squeezing the excess glue back into the bowl.

4. Drape the yarn over the inflated balloon. Drape more lengths of yarn over the balloon, layering pieces over one another and leaving the bottom of the balloon (a few inches around the tied end) bare.

5. Set aside to dry completely. When dry, pop the balloon with a straight pin and carefully remove.

Careful,
She Bites

YOU
MATTER

Love

LET-IT-POUR PROJECTS

What a Card!

Of all the craft projects, this one has the most freedom—because you're the artist who's making all of the choices. Remember: There are no rules!

WHAT YOU NEED

blank cards
magazines
scissors
textured paper
construction paper
tape (cellophane,
    double-sided,
    and duct)
glue sticks

Optional add-ons

acrylic paints
crayons
hole punches
markers
newspapers
pressed flowers
sponges
spray paints
stamps
stapler
stencils
stickers

HOW TO MAKE

1. Gather the supplies you want to use. Start with a blank card in a favorite color and begin designing.

2. Cut or tear images, backgrounds, and words from magazines. Find a range of shades that go with the color you've chosen and see how they work on your blank card.

3. Use colored construction or textured paper to frame an image or photo.

4. For a textured look, tape materials directly on card. For a neater look, use a glue stick or double-sided tape.

5. To make a more elaborate personal statement, add stickers, pressed flowers, stamps, punches, or whatever you like.

6. Create themed cards by picking colors, expressions, and images that capture a holiday or sentiment.

Magical Beans Mosaic

Bull's-eye! We know beans are good for you, but these legumes lift your spirits in a creative way. Compose a bold target or checkerboard squares with bags of beans and glue, making your project as teensy or gigantic as you want.

WHAT YOU NEED

- pencil
- canvas boards
- small paintbrush
- craft glue
- dried beans
- ruler

HOW TO MAKE

1. Start by drawing a pattern in pencil on your board. Our mosaics have geometric designs, but you can do a still life or even a portrait in dried beans—think of this as a color-by-numbers painting.

2. "Paint" a thin layer of glue in one area of your pattern, and sprinkle the area with colorful beans. To keep the look graphic, use a single color in each area.

3. Use the ruler to tidy up the edges of the beans before moving on to the next area.

4. Repeat Steps 1 through 3 until the board is covered. Let dry for 1 hour.

Peekaboo Puppet Show

Let the show begin! Decorate this cardboard theater in the most cheerful colors imaginable. Add a printed curtain, and set the stage with a cast of clay characters. Bravo!

WHAT YOU NEED

- large box
- X-Acto knife
- tempera paint
- medium paintbrush
- scissors
- fabric
- packing or masking tape
- pipe cleaners
- stickers (optional)

HOW TO MAKE

1. GROWN-UPS: Cut out a large square in the front of the box with the knife. Scallop the top edge of the box.

2. Paint the outside of the box with bright tempera paint and let dry. Apply another coat of paint; let dry completely.

3. Cut one piece of fabric that covers the whole window, then cut it in half. Tape the top edges of one half along the inside upper edge of the opening to form a curtain. Repeat on the other side.

4. GROWN-UPS: Using the knife, poke a small hole on each side. Thread a pipe cleaner through each hole, gather the curtain, and twist each pipe cleaner's ends together to create tiebacks. Trim excess.

5. Decorate the box with bright stickers, or paint contrasting dots on the scallops in the front.

Clay Nation Friends

Imagine characters to star in your first show—and then fashion them out of clay. Be sure to give them silly names too!

Crayola Model Magic, Fimo, or Sculpey clay (available at art-supply and craft stores)
colored pencils

1 Mold characters out of clay, making sure they're sturdy enough to sit on a pencil without falling apart. Add little details to bring the characters alive—bright eyes, big grins, and stripes and buttons for the little people; whiskers and a pet collar on a kitty cat.

2 Place puppet securely on the eraser end of the pencil; let dry overnight.

Oink! Meow! Glove Puppets

These sassy creatures can be made using an old pair of gloves or a stray mitten. (Now you know why you keep 'em!)

WHAT YOU NEED

For pig

  knit glove in light pink
  dark pink felt
  scissors
  tacky craft glue
2 small black pom-poms
2 tiny black pom-poms
  black squeeze paint
  pink pipe cleaner
  pencil

For cat

  knit glove in dark pink
    (or any color of your choice)
  white felt
  scissors
  tacky craft glue
  black string or yarn
  small white pom-pom
  black squeeze paint

HOW TO MAKE

For pig

1. Cut a circle and 2 small triangles of pink felt and glue to the palm of the glove for the nose and ears.

2. Glue the small black pom-poms on for eyes and the tiny black pom-poms onto the nose for nostrils. With the black squeeze paint, paint in the mouth.

3. Cut the pipe cleaner in half and twist around a pencil. Remove twist and glue to the back of the glove. Let dry.

For cat

1. Cut 2 eye shapes and two small triangles for ears from the white felt. Glue in place. Cut small pieces of the black string or yarn for whiskers; glue onto the glove. Glue the white pom-pom on top of them for the nose.

2. Using the black squeeze paint, mark in the eyes and mouth details.

Mad Scientist Experiment

This crystal garden takes only a few minutes to set up and will entertain you for weeks. Check it out daily to see how crystals form, but don't touch it or you might disturb the process.

WHAT YOU NEED

	freezer bag
6 TO 8	charcoal briquettes
	hammer
	small bowl
	distilled water
	Pyrex glass bowl or pie plate
	jar with an airtight lid
1 c	ammonia
1 c, plus 2 T	non-iodized salt
1½ c	laundry bluing
	food coloring

HOW TO MAKE

1 Put charcoal briquettes in a freezer bag and, using a hammer, break up into chunks about 1 in. in size. Transfer chunks to a bowl and cover with distilled water. When briquettes are completely saturated (tiny bubbles will stop floating to the surface), drain off the excess water and transfer pieces to the shallower Pyrex bowl or pie plate.

2 Using a jar with an airtight lid, combine ammonia, salt, and laundry bluing. Mix well. Pour about half the mixture over the briquettes and then cover jar with the airtight lid until you need it again.

3 Scatter drops of food coloring over the charcoal. Sprinkle on 2 T salt.

4 Set your project aside in a safe place (away from pets). Check it every day to see the progress. When the bottom of the bowl is dry, add a little more of the mixture. Remember to shake up your mixture, because it may have settled a bit. Be careful not to pour over the top, as the crystals are fragile.

GROWN-UPS: The mixture, which contains dissolved salt, is drawn up through the pores in the charcoal briquettes and evaporates, leaving behind layer upon layer of salt-crystal formations. This intriguing process continues until all the liquid evaporates. The colors come from the liquid absorbing the drops of food coloring on its way up.

Cookie Cutter Candles

Light up a room by transforming plain candles into cool-looking ones. Decorate white pillars with cookie cutter cutouts of colored beeswax.

WHAT YOU NEED

cookie cutters
sheets of colored beeswax
pillar candles in various sizes
tacky craft glue
sewing pins or map pins (with little
  balls on the ends)

HOW TO MAKE

1. Using the cookie cutters, cut shapes out of the different colors of beeswax.

2. Apply to the candles using the tacky glue. Secure with a pin.

3. Check for any drips while drying.

4. When dry, pull out the pins.

NOTE: Never leave lit candles unattended.

Pushpin Pillars

Here is the simplest project that gets the neatest results—just add a little flower power to plain pillar candles with colorful pushpins.

WHAT YOU NEED

pillar candles in different colors
pushpins
map pins
thumbtacks
scrapbooking brads, grommets, or cutouts

HOW TO MAKE

1. Decorate the candles using the materials above by pushing the scrapbooking brads, grommets, or cutouts into the candle using your thumb.

NOTE: Never leave lit candles unattended.

We're Forever Blowing Bubbles

Bet you didn't know that you can make the prettiest-looking patterns by blowing bubbles!

WHAT YOU NEED

For each color

2 t	dishwashing liquid
3 T	water
¼ c	powdered tempera paint
	spoon
	clean jar with lid
	bubble pipe
	white paper

HOW TO MAKE

1. Mix dishwashing liquid, water, and paint in the jar with a spoon. Blend it well by tightening the lid on the jar and shaking. Continue to add more paint to darken color.

2. Pour a little bit of the mixture into a bubble pipe and blow bubbles onto white paper. (Be sure not to sip in the mixture or inhale it because you could get sick.) Let them dry into circle patterns. After the bubbles dry, overlap with another color of bubble paint for a more layered effect.

Shower Slime

Don't mind the name: Whip up a batch of this super-cool gel and you'll have no problem cleaning up your act. P.S. It smells really fresh too.

WHAT YOU NEED

3 c	distilled water
6 T	unscented shampoo concentrate saucepan
3 t	salt
25 drops	citrus essential oil
6 drops	green food coloring plastic squeeze bottle with a cap

HOW TO MAKE

1 GROWN-UPS: You need to supervise this step, as it involves the stove. Warm up the water and shampoo concentrate in saucepan over medium heat for a few minutes until completely dissolved.

2 Stir salt, citrus oil, and food coloring into the saucepan, blending it well until the consistency is a bit thick, about 3 minutes; let cool. Store in a plastic squeeze bottle with a cap.

Fun-in-the-Tub Bars

Rub-a-dub-dub these eye-popping bars into existence by stirring food coloring (and yummy-smelling oils) into melted glycerin soap.

WHAT YOU NEED

For 5 bars of orange soap

5 (4-oz.) bars	unscented glycerin soap double boiler
25 drops	orange oil
5 drops	orange food coloring
10 T	heavy whipping cream
25 drops	vanilla fragrance oil
5 (5-oz.)	soap molds (available at craft stores)

HOW TO MAKE

1 GROWN-UPS: These first two steps involve heating up soap at the stove, so no matter how old your children are, it's best if you're close at hand. Melt the soap in a double boiler over low heat until it's pourable, about 15 minutes.

2 Remove pan from heat. One at a time, mix in orange oil, food coloring, cream, and vanilla fragrance oil until mixture is thoroughly blended.

3 Pour the liquid into molds and let it harden for a day.

4 Remove soaps from molds and lather up!

To make Lime Citrus Soap, substitute 25 drops lime fragrance oil for orange oil, 5 drops green food coloring for orange food coloring, and omit vanilla fragrance oil.

Exploding Soap Bombs

Have a blast making these fizzy balls in a rainbow of colors. Measure carefully and take your time when removing the soap from the scoop so that it remains solid. You want it to make a sweet explosion when it hits the bathwater!

WHAT YOU NEED

2¼ c baking soda
1 c citric acid
1 c cornstarch
  bowls, large and small
  essential oils
  food coloring
  mister filled with water or witch hazel
  small ice cream scoop
  waxed paper

HOW TO MAKE

1. Mix baking soda, citric acid, and cornstarch in a large bowl.

2. Remove ½ c of the mixture and place in the small bowl. Set the big bowl aside for later. In the small bowl, add a few drops of fragrance oils and food coloring to create the scent and color you want. Mix well.

3. Remove another ½ c of mixture and add to mixture in small bowl. Lightly mist with the water or witch hazel to add a little moisture so the mixture will stick together. Be conservative: If you add too much liquid, the salts will start to fizz.

4. Using a small ice cream scoop, mold soap bomb balls, gently pressing them into shape. The balls might be a bit fragile, so be careful as you transfer them to a piece of waxed paper.

5. Go back to the large bowl and take out another ½ c of the mixture and repeat Steps 2 through 4 until you have used up all the dry mixture.

6. Let soap bombs dry overnight on waxed paper.

Any of the following 10 projects work well for a spur-of-the-moment activity. They're simple and the supplies needed are things you probably have on hand. Another plus: You can do them year-round (there's nothing holiday specific about them). From writing messages in invisible ink to pressing flowers, these truly cool crafts will delight all ages.

Silliest Putty Ever

It acts just like the stuff you buy in the store: It bounces! Plus, you can stretch it and transfer your favorite newspaper comic strip onto it.

WHAT YOU NEED

	small bowl
	spoon
1 c	white glue
	food coloring
1 c	liquid starch
	airtight plastic container

HOW TO MAKE

1. Mix the glue and a few drops of food coloring in bowl.

2. Stir in the liquid starch a little at a time, until the mixture starts to gel. Keep stirring until mixture gets thick and sticky enough to shape into a ball. Store in airtight plastic container.

Secret Messages

Ssssh! Kids like the secretive nature of sending an undercover note to a pal—and getting one too. Here's how to do both.

WHAT YOU NEED

FOR SECRET MESSAGES

	waxed paper
2	sheets of white paper
	pencil
	highlighter or crayon

HOW TO MAKE

1. Place a piece of waxed paper between 2 sheets of white paper. Using the pencil, write your message.

2. Destroy the top page and waxed paper, as all good spies would do.

3. To view the messages, use a highlighter or crayon to highlight the "invisible" writing on the remaining piece of paper.

WHAT YOU NEED

FOR INVISIBLE INK

One lemon (or ReaLemon 100% Lemon Juice from Concentrate)
small paintbrush
plain paper

HOW TO MAKE

1. Squeeze the lemon (or pour ¼ c ReaLemon 100% Lemon Juice) into a small bowl.

2. With a small brush, write a message using the juice. When the juice dries, the message disappears.

3. To reveal the message, hold the paper up to the sun or near a lightbulb (the warmth turns the dried lemon juice brown).

Two-Way Photo

You'll feel like an illusionist when you pull off this magic trick. The transformation of your two photos won't make sense at first, but as soon as this craft is finished, you'll think, "Aha!"

2   contrasting 8 x 10-in. photographs
      (color copy enlargements work best)
    ruler
    pencil
    scissors (or paper cutter)
    large piece of construction paper
    paper glue
    mat board

HOW TO MAKE

1   On the back of the photos, draw vertical lines ½ in. apart, using the ruler.

2   Number the strips lightly in pencil on the back, from right to left. Neatly cut out the strips. Keep the strips from each picture separate.

3   Spread a thin layer of paper glue on the back of strip #1 and place strip #1 on construction paper; then place strip #1 from the second picture next to it.

4   Repeat Step 3 for all the strips. This project may look like a mess, but don't worry—you are not done yet. Allow the project to dry completely. Trim construction paper, leaving a 1-in. border on left and right edges.

5   Fold along the edges of each strip to create an accordion pleat. You should see the effect beginning to happen.

6   Mount the accordion-pleated paper onto the mat board by gluing right and left edges in place.

7   Once dry, your artwork is ready for hanging. The best location for your finished product is a hallway. When you walk down the hallway the picture reveals one side; on your way back, you will see the other.

Flower Drying

Pros use silica gel to dry flowers. But for home use, it's easier—and safer (silica gel contains dopants, which are poisonous to eat) to make a batch of cornmeal and borax (a laundry booster found next to detergents at the grocery store).

WHAT YOU NEED

- **1 c** powdered borax
- **2 c** cornmeal
- shoebox
- fresh flowers

HOW TO MAKE

1. Mix powdered borax and cornmeal.

2. Pour 1 in. of the mixture into the bottom of a shoebox.

3. Trim stems of flowers to about 1 in. in length.

4. Place flowers facedown in the box. Carefully pour the mixture around the sides of the flowers and over them until they're covered by approximately 1 in. of the mixture.

5. Set the box aside to sit at room temperature for 3 to 4 weeks.

Pressed Flowers

You'll get the best results if you use small flowers with thin stems: Pansies are the easiest, but lavender and heather work well too. Use this simple do-it-yourself method or try flower-pressing kits available at your local craft store.

WHAT YOU NEED

- heavy books
- waxed paper
- paper towels
- cut flowers

HOW TO MAKE

1. Tear off a piece of waxed paper twice the size of a page from your book. Fold in half.

2. Open to the center of the book and slip the waxed paper inside. This will protect your book from any moisture that may come from the pressed flowers.

3. Place a paper towel between the waxed paper pages and arrange your flowers so that they do not touch.

4. Cover the arrangement with another paper towel and carefully close the book.

5. Stack a few more books on top. Let it sit for a couple of days, so flowers press flat.

Kitchen Clay

Here are three easy recipes for clay—just look in your pantry for the ingredients.

For cornstarch clay
    medium saucepan
    spoon
1 c   salt
⅓ c   water
½ c   cornstarch
¼ c   cold water

HOW TO MAKE

1. In a medium saucepan, mix salt and water over medium heat, stirring occasionally for about 3 to 4 minutes.

2. Remove from heat and add cornstarch and cold water. Stir until mixture thickens, then knead. If it is too sticky, add a little more cornstarch.

3. Store in a sealed container with a piece of damp sponge for up to 2 weeks.

WHAT YOU NEED

For cooked-flour clay
    medium saucepan
    spoon
1 c   all-purpose flour
1 c   water
2 t   cream of tartar
¼ c   salt
1 T   vegetable oil
    food coloring
    waxed paper

HOW TO MAKE

1. In a medium saucepan, mix all the ingredients. Cook over medium heat, stirring constantly. When dough becomes hard to stir and sticks to spoon (about 5 minutes), transfer to waxed paper.

2. Cool until able to handle and knead 10 to 15 times until smooth.

3. Store in a sealed container with a piece of damp sponge for up to 2 weeks.

WHAT YOU NEED

For baking soda clay
    medium saucepan
    spoon
2 c   baking soda
1 c   cornstarch
1¼ c water

HOW TO MAKE

1. In a medium saucepan, stir the baking soda, cornstarch, and water. Cook over medium heat, stirring constantly, until mixture resembles mashed potatoes.

2. Place in a bowl and cover with a damp cloth until cool.

3. Store in a sealed container.

Homemade Finger Paint

In a pinch, this do-it-yourself paint will work for an afternoon of finger painting fun. GROWN-UPS: Kids will end up with colorful paws, but some warm water will come to the rescue.

WHAT YOU NEED

	medium microwave-safe bowl
2 T	sugar
½ c	cornstarch
2 c	cold water
¼ c	clear dishwashing liquid
	food coloring

HOW TO MAKE

1. In microwave-safe bowl, mix the sugar and cornstarch together. Slowly add cold water until the dry mixture is completely saturated.

2. Microwave on low heat for 1 minute or until the mixture becomes an almost-clear gel. Set aside to cool.

3. When your mixture is cool, stir in clear dishwashing liquid.

4. Divide the mixture into separate containers and add coloring.

Sticker Glue

Who doesn't like playing with stickers? Here's how to make a nontoxic glue that will transform favorite pictures into stickers. GROWN-UPS: You'll need to help the kids with this activity, but the results will wow them.

WHAT YOU NEED

	pictures
	scissors
1	pack unflavored gelatin
1 T	cold water
3 T	boiling water
½ t	white corn syrup
½ t	lemon extract
	small paintbrush

HOW TO MAKE

1. Cut pictures from your favorite magazines.

2. Dissolve the gelatin in cold water.

3. Add boiling water and mix well.

4. Add corn syrup and lemon extract and mix well.

5. Using a small paintbrush, cover the back of your cutouts with the gelatin mixture. Let dry.

6. Lick to activate, just the way you would a stamp.

Goo & Slime

Yes—the words sound icky, but that's what is great about goo and slime. And kids will love making batches of it to surprise friends when they come over to goof around.

For goo

    small bowls
8 oz. white glue
1 c water, separated
    spoon
    green food coloring
1 T powdered borax
    airtight container

1. Mix glue and ¾ c water in a bowl with spoon. Add a few drops of green food coloring; mix well.

2. In another bowl, mix borax and ¼ c water.

3. Add borax mixture to glue mixture and stir until it forms a blob. Store in airtight container.

For slime

    bowl
    spoon
2 c water
1 c cornstarch
    food coloring
    airtight container

1. Mix the cornstarch and water until the mixture becomes pasty.

2. Add food coloring a few drops at a time and stir in. Store in airtight container.

Fake Blood

OK, it's a little gruesome. But scary sleepovers just won't be the same if you don't have some fun with this simply ghastly concoction! (It's also a lifesaver—no pun intended—for impromptu All Hallow's Eve getups.)

    bowl
    spoon
2 c water
½ c cornstarch
    red food coloring
    airtight container

1. Mix water and cornstarch until mixture has a syrupy texture.

2. Add red food coloring a few drops at a time and stir. Add more if needed. Store in an airtight container.

Templates

Create templates for crafts by
enlarging these to the desired size
by copying onto graph paper or
enlarging on a copy machine.

Crazy Carrot Party Bags
from page 38
1 square equals 2 in.
(enlarge 200%)

A-tisket, A-tasket Basket
from page 40
1 square equals 2 in.
(enlarge to desired size)

Miss Lazy Daisy
from page 112
1 square equals 4 in.
(enlarge 400%)
Flowerpot size varies
from child to child

Jack-o'-Lanterns
from page 96
1 square equals 2 in.
(enlarge 200%)

Falling Leaves Banner
from page 126
1 square equals 2 in.
(enlarge 200%)

Best Places for Craft Supplies

ART & CRAFT

A.C. Moore
www.acmoore.com

Art Supply Warehouse
www.aswexpress.com

Craft Catalog
www.craftcatalog.com

Crayola
www.crayolastore.com

Dick Blick
www.dickblick.com

Elmer's
www.elmers.com

Jo-Ann Fabrics
www.joann.com

Michael's
www.michaels.com

Pearl Paint
www.pearlpaint.com

Plaid
www.plaidonline.com

Quality Shells
www.qualityshells.com

Sunshine Discount Crafts
www.sunshinecrafts.com

BEADS & JEWELRY MAKING

Beadbox
www.beadbox.com

CANDLE & SOAP MAKING

Aztec International
www.candlemaking.com

Magic Cabin
www.magiccabin.com

Yaley Enterprises
www.yaley.com

CANDIES

Wilton Industries
www.wilton.com

Yummies
www.yummies.com

CLOTHING & DYES

Dharma Trading Co.
www.dharmatrading.com

Pro Chemical and Dye
www.prochemical.com

DRIED FLOWERS

The Flower Mart
www.theflowermart.com

Nature's Pressed Flowers
www.naturespressed.com

HALLOWEEN

Funkins Artificial Pumpkins
www.funkins.com

Halloween Online
www.pumpkincarving101.com

MOSAIC & GLASS

Delphi
www.delphiglass.com

Mosaic Mercantile
www.mosaicmerc.com

Wit's End Mosaic
www.mosaic-witsend.com

PAPER

Kate's Paperie
www.katespaperie.com

ROAD SIGNS

Google Image Search
www.images.google.com

SEWING

Newark Dressmaker Supply
www.newarkdress.com

OTHER

Home Goods
www.homegoods.com
Garden ornaments for bird feeder

IKEA
www.ikea.com
Small wooden chests, frames, glass votives, and plates

Mrs. Stewart Bluing
www.mrsstewart.com
Whitening products

Pottery Barn
www.potterybarn.com
Frames, glass votives, and plates

Queen & Company
www.queenandcompany.com
Brads for candlemaking

Staples
www.staples.com
Ball pushpins for decorating candles

And don't forget to visit Rosie's Crafty U online for more fun tips and craft ideas.
www.rosie.com

thank you to all the people who helped me create this book

Bobby Pearce: He can make a chandelier out of a piece of tissue paper and a hanger.
Doug Turshen: Creative Director extraordinaire who pulled it all together.
David Huang and Steve Turner: Perfect graphic design.
Thaddeus Buckley: An artist!
Donna Bulseco: For helping to make all the directions easy to follow.
Sarah Wharton: Who knows where the commas go.

Amy Leonard and Matthew Mead: Making each project look so good.
Laura Martin, Charlotte Lyons, and Ellen Goldberg: For some clever ideas.
Heidi Safer: For her delicious Chocolate Eggs.

All the talented photographers:
Antonis Achilleos, Monica Buck, Reed Davis, Colleen Duffley, Miki Duisterhof, John Kernick, Charles Maraia, Tara Sgroi, Daniela Stallinger, Mark Thomas and Frank Veronsky.

Robert Barnett: For his legal expertise.
Sharon de Gier and the whole team at KidRo Productions.
And last but not least, **Amanda Murray** and all the folks at Simon & Schuster.

PHOTOGRAPHY

Antonis Achilleos: Pages 17, 19, 22, 23, 27, 28, 29, 42, 44, 76, 77, 88, 89, 91, 106, 107, 109, 123, 124, 125, 127, 128, 141, 143, 144, 145, 147, 149, 150, 151, 161, 164, 165, 166, 167, 169, 170, 171, 172, 173, 181, 183, 184, 185, 186, 187

Monica Buck: Pages 57, 58, 59

Reed Davis: Pages 2, 24, 25, 32, 33, 34, 35, 37, 39, 41, 50, 51, 52, 53, 61, 63, 64, 67, 69, 71, 73, 83, 87, 97, 101, 102, 103, 111, 112, 115, 135, 175, 177, 179, 205

Colleen Duffley: Pages 78, 188, 189, 191, 193

Miki Duisterhof: Pages 47, 49, 80, 81, 82, 84, 85

John Kernick: Pages 116, 118, 121, 152, 153, 154, 155, 156, 158, 159, 168

Charles Maraia: Pages 131, 137, 139

Tara Sgroi: Pages 94, 99, 100, 105

Daniela Stallinger: Pages 5, 11, 13, 15, 74,

Mark Thomas: Page 104

Frank Veronsky: Front cover, page 207

ILLUSTRATIONS

Thaddeus Buckley: Pages 3, 9, 21, 31, 55, 93, 129, 163

Steve Turner: Pages 68, 80, 134, 200, 201, 202, 203